Finding the Root

Digging Deep To Uproot The Shame Holding You Back

EMILY EHE

Copyright © 2021 by Emily Ehe

Finding the Root

All rights reserved. No part of this publication may be reproduced, distributed, or transmitted in any form or by any means, including photocopying, recording, or other electronic or mechanical methods, without the prior written permission of the publisher, except in the case of brief quotations embodied in critical reviews and certain other noncommercial uses permitted by copyright law. For permission requests, write to the publisher, addressed "Attention: Permissions Coordinator," at info@beyondpublishing.net

Quantity sales special discounts are available on quantity purchases by corporations, associations, and others. For details, contact the publisher at the address above.

Orders by U.S. and Canada trade bookstores and wholesalers. Email info@ BeyondPublishing.net

The Beyond Publishing Speakers Bureau can bring authors to your live event. For more information or to book an event contact the Beyond Publishing Speakers Bureau speak@BeyondPublishing.net

The Author can be reached directly at info@BeyondPublishing.net

Manufactured and printed in the United States of America distributed globally by BeyondPublishing.net

New York | Los Angeles | London | Sydney

ISBN Hardcover: 978-1-637922-42-2

This book is dedicated to all the people out there who have tried *everything they can think of* and found nothing that worked. They are left thinking all hope is lost... it is not.

ACKNOWLEDGEMENTS

First and foremost, thank you to my husband, Pierre, for always believing in me, supporting me, and planting the seed in me years ago to write a book.

Thank you to my cousin, Scott Esbeck, for the amazing cover design.

Thank you, Mary Steinhoff, Clare Crowson, Kristen Cook, Kristi Rike, and Maggie Sample, for your feedback at various points along the way.

I couldn't have done it without all of you and your feedback, love, support and encouragement throughout the process.

TABLE OF CONTENTS

Introduction 7

Chapter 1: Healing is Possible 11

PART 1
WHAT IS A TOXIC SHAME, AND HOW DO I KNOW IF I STRUGGLE WITH IT

Chapter 2: Did You Know you Might Be Super Human? 21

Chapter 3: Symptoms Of Toxic Shame 33

PART 2
WHERE DOES TOXIC SHAME COME FROM?

Chapter 4; The Origin Of Shame 55

PART 3
WHY YOU CAN'T IGNORE IT ANY LONGER?

Chapter 5: The Fruit Of Toxic Shame 65

PART 4
HOW DO I FIND THE ROOT

Chapter 6: Watch Your Thoughts 77

Chapter 7: Listen TO What You Tell Yourself 87

PART 5
HOW DO I HEAL FROM TOXIC SHAME

Chapter 8: Expose It 101

Chapter 9: Give Yourself And Others Permission To Be Human 107

PART 6
HOW DO I MOVE FORWARD &
MAINTAIN MY GROWTH

Chapter 10: Keeping Shame Healthy 121

INTRODUCTION

You may be asking right now: "*Who is Emily Ehe? I've never heard of her. Why should I read her book?*"

Well, let me answer that for you. I'm a small-town Iowa girl, with two younger brothers. I was homeschooled all the way through school, until I got to high school. I attended the local high school for Spanish, keyboarding, and accounting classes. This was where I fell in love with Spanish and went on to major in Spanish at college. Post college, I moved to Des Moines, Iowa and worked for a couple of different insurance companies. In one of said companies, I worked as a bilingual customer service representative. About five years after college graduation, I got a job in Korea, where I was assigned to teach English as a second language. It was the toughest time of my life, until marriage, and after just one year, I moved back to the States. I relocated to Dallas, TX and it was shortly after this that I found myself on a giant stage, sharing the story of God's grace in my life.

I'm just a regular everyday person, like you, that has struggled with toxic shame. Toxic shame is a feeling of worthlessness, stemming from a painful belief in one's personal defectiveness. Oftentimes, toxic shame is developed when someone says something critical or treats you poorly, and as a result, you - knowingly or unknowingly - use that experience to create a negative belief about yourself. This shame is either a direct result of experiences we've been shaped by as adults, or events that happened to us in childhood. Despite that toxic shame is prevalent in our society, it is not something we often hear or talk about. This is rather unfortunate, because one of the ways to heal toxic shame is to talk about it.

By virtue of God's grace, help and healing, I have been given victory over toxic shame. I'm not an expert in psychology, or a counselor or a mental health professional of any kind, I am just someone who has spent a lot of time healing from toxic shame. For this reason, I'm here to share my journey and all I've learned from it with you.

Healing looks different for everyone, but I'd like to share a glimpse of what healing has looked like for me. I owe a part of my healing process to reading books that provided timely insights that I needed at precise moments. Some other parts of this process have come from sharing my struggles with safe friends who encouraged me and spoke into my life along the way. God pointed me to exceptional counselors to help me unpack, process, and make sense of my past, and understand how it relates to my present. Another portion of my healing journey can be linked to Re:generation, a 12-step Christ-centered recovery program. This program helps many people find freedom from all sorts of struggles, such as fear, anger, substance abuse and co-dependency.

I am a Christ-follower and so, I'm writing from a Biblical perspective, but the things I'm saying here can be applied, whether you love Jesus or not. If you don't, I hope that you come to know Jesus personally while reading this book. He is AMAZING! He knows us better than we know ourselves, as He is the one who created us. He can give you strength when you have exhausted yours.

After this transformational journey and a couple people's nudging, I felt compelled to share my story with others, and now that you know a little bit about me, let's go to Chapter One, where I open by sharing my story of God's grace in my life in front of hundreds of people!

CHAPTER 1

HEALING IS POSSIBLE

Getting up on that stage was a surreal moment—a time I'll never forget. Leading up to that point, I remember thinking, *Is this really me? Is this really happening? Wow, I've come so far. I never thought I could do something like this!*

I thought back to the little girl I once was. I hated being on a stage in front of people; I would have done anything to avoid it. While waiting for my turn at piano recitals, my hands would simultaneously be cold and sweaty, and my breathing, shallow. I was so nervous that afterwards, I could barely remember being on stage or recall how I sounded. Everything in the performance would be a blur to me.

Years later, in college, I took a compulsory public speaking class, and the entire time, I could not wait for it to be over for the semester. I didn't understand why anyone would be required to take such a class. I mean, who needs to take a class like that, when they *never intend* to speak in front of people?

Can anyone else relate? Throughout my college years, mandatory presentations were always dreaded assignments. Afterwards, my friends would ask me how I did, and I would not be able to respond, because my experiences were usually a blur, just as it had been when

I was younger. I hope this gives you a picture of just how much I *HATED* public speaking.

But now, this same person who had struggled with speaking publicly throughout her life, even in a small group setting, was now approaching a stage to speak to a *large* audience. I was preparing to share the story of God's grace in my life from the same stage where well-known speakers like Joni Erickson Tada, Nic Vojick, John Piper, Randy Alcorn, and others had shared *their* stories; a stage where musicians like Shane and Shane, and Phil Wickham have sung.

I was preparing to share some of my most vulnerable experiences with a few hundred people, most of whom were strangers. I was nervous, but much less nervous than I expected to be. I don't share this to brag about myself, but to show you just how far God had already brought me in my healing journey. For me, it was a miracle.

At this point in my life, I had not yet learned that toxic shame was largely responsible for my avoidance of public speaking. But the whole time, God knew, and He used this experience as part of my healing process. At this juncture, I feel like it's important for me to point out that not all people who dread public speaking suffer from toxic shame. But for me, it was the root of my fear; if I wasn't certain that I could do something well, I would avoid doing it entirely, in order to evade the possibility of public embarrassment and emotional discomfort that would last for days afterwards. I also had a deep-seated belief that everyone was judging me and picking apart my every move and mistake.

When I signed up to lead a group of girls through Re:generation (a 12-step program for finding healing in Christ from hurts, habits, and hang-ups), I knew that it would mean sharing my story from the stage for the large group session. But because God had used Re:generation so much in my own life and I believed He was leading me, I was willing to step outside my comfort zone. I didn't want fear to prevent me from being obedient.

Re:generation had taught me that it wasn't just *my* story that I was sharing, but *God's* story of His grace in my life. It was a story that God could use to encourage and bring hope to others. I knew that if He was leading me to do it, He would see me through it, and He did. Having personal, tangible experiences of God showing up for me in the past gave me confidence to share the story of His grace in my life, even on a stage, in front of a few hundred people.

Now it was time to walk up onto the stage, and I was just hoping that I wouldn't trip up the stairs. *Phew! I made it to the podium safely.* I set my papers down and put my hands on the podium in hopes to hide the fact that they were shaking. I also chose to sit rather than stand, so as to make it less obvious that my legs were shaking. I began to speak, and slowly, my nervousness dissipated. My voice was normalizing quickly. I was getting into a rhythm. Before I knew it, I had finished sharing my story of God's redemption in my life, and was walking off the stage. It had gone smoothly, without a hitch, and I was grateful and happy. *Wow, I did it!*

Afterwards, people walked up to me, commending me on how natural I sounded, adding that I made it look easy. I was shocked. I thought it was apparent that I was nervous. *Wait, what? I looked and sounded like a natural?* That was a compliment that was incredibly meaningful to me. I was mind-blown. I realized that despite the nerves, I actually kind of enjoyed it. *Wait, what? Did I really just think that?*

I would like to share another instance of how healing from toxic shame led me outside of my comfort zone. I recently co-authored a book entitled, "Finding Diamonds." My chapter of the book was on the topic of the importance of how we think. Even just a few years ago, I would never have thought that I would be capable of sharing my story publicly, under any circumstances, at any point in my life! People can be cruel, and as a recovering queen of self-protection, I would have feared that it could open me up to attacks and criticisms. But for God, I would not have had the confidence, courage, and healing to put myself out there like that. God is the God of the impossible. He can do the unimaginable with us.

Fast forward to when I had the opportunity to discuss, on a podcast, my chapter in the book, "Finding Diamonds" I immediately agreed to it. *Wait, who is this person who volunteered to speak on a podcast? Do I know her? Wow, God has brought her this far!* In the days leading up to the podcast, I was so comfortable that I often found myself forgetting that I needed to prepare. In the moments just before the podcast started, while I was waiting for the link to join to be sent, I realized I was barely nervous. My body wasn't shaking. My breathing was normal. My hands weren't cold and sweaty at the same time. I noticed that as I talked, my voice was steady. It was hard to recognize myself — I mean that in a good way.

It is amazing what God can do in your life if you let Him. I don't share these stories to say, "Look at me!" Instead, I hope to encourage you by telling you that if *I* can do it, you can, too. You are capable of more than you ever thought possible, if you rid yourself of your toxic shame.

I still wouldn't say that it comes naturally for me to "put myself out there," but the more I heal, the easier it gets. Throughout my healing journey, God has given me a passion for being healthy emotionally, physically and spiritually. I'm passionate about encouraging and helping people who are wounded and hurting to heal, because I've experienced firsthand how lonely it is to be hurting and be afraid that things will not improve. I also know how difficult healing can be, but I can also testify that it is rewarding and lifegiving!

I don't want to keep God's story of grace and redemption in my life to myself. It's not mine; it's His and I'm just a steward of it. I'm reminded of 2 Corinthians 1:3-4, "Blessed be the God and Father of our Lord Jesus Christ, the Father of mercies and God of all comfort, who comforts us in all our affliction, so that we may be able to comfort those who are in any affliction, with the comfort with which we ourselves are comforted by God." God has given me comfort, and I'm here to pass it on to you.

Right about now, you might be thinking, *this sounds too good to be true.* I get that. I've been in your shoes and would have thought the same a short while ago. When I made the decision to attend Re:generation, I felt that it was my last hope at change. Up until then, I had done everything I knew how to do.

I had prayed, memorized Scripture, targeted to the issues I was struggling with, and tried hard over and over to rid myself of some of my hurts, habits, and hang-ups. Up until that point, it had all been to no avail, so I get it if you are skeptical. When I got to Re:generation,

I had heard of how God could transform you through the program and bring healing. During the program, each week, I heard stories of dramatic transformation in people's lives. They told us that *you get out what you put in.*

I knew I'd put 110% into the program, but feared I would be unsuccessful and come out with 0% transformation, freedom, or victory. I'm here to tell you that my fear was a lie from the pit of hell. I'm not the exception who always fails, and neither are YOU!

I also want to let you know that everyone's healing journey looks different, so, please don't compare your progress to someone else's. Flowers in the garden bloom in their own time. They don't compare themselves to the flower next door and think they are a failure because they don't look like that yet. Therefore, don't be discouraged if it takes longer than you expect. It might, and that's okay.

When I completed Re:generation, I thought, *Wow! I'm so free!* I experienced so much progress, growth, transformation, and freedom in my life. I returned a year later and led a group of girls through the program, where God revealed more layers of my heart. It was amazing!

Shortly after that, I sensed that God wanted me to go see a counselor. I pushed back. Waited. Questioned. Resisted. I thought, *God, I'm healthier than a lot of people I know already, thanks to Re:generation. You've brought so much healing, and I'm grateful! Is this really You? Is there more that I need to do?* I fought it off for a while until I knew it had to be God's leading. I think the biggest reason that I resisted was because I thought God's leading meant that I was really messed up if after two rounds of Re:generation, I *still* needed counseling.

But God broke through my pride and toxic shame, and brought even deeper healing through counseling. I wouldn't trade it for the world!

Brené Brown, one of my favorite authors, is a research professor at the University of Houston, who has spent two decades studying shame, empathy, vulnerability and courage. She has many powerful quotes on shame. I want to wrap up this chapter with two quotes from her that I've seen going around on social media.

"Shame corrodes the very part of us that believes we are capable of change." [1]

"Owning our story and loving ourselves through the process is one of the bravest things we'll ever do." [2]

Don't let toxic shame keep you from believing that you are capable of changing, growing, becoming free and truly living! I want to encourage you to be gentle with yourself through the process. My former counselor, Damaris, encouraged me to accept all the different parts of me. It was a new concept for me for sure. I had never thought about accepting the parts of me that I didn't like. She explained to me that all parts of me served a purpose and had a role to play in my life. I'd like you to consider the possibility of accepting yourself, deeply and completely, as you are, and not as you ought to be. What do you think?

---

1 Brown, Brené. *Daring Greatly: How the Courage to Be Vulnerable Transforms the Way We Live, Love, Parent, and Lead.* London: Penguin, 2015.

2 Brown, Brené. *The Gifts of Imperfection: Let Go of Who You Think You're Supposed to Be and Embrace Who You Are.* Hazelden Publishing, 2010.

Action Steps—Please take some time to consider if you accept yourself deeply and completely as you are and not as you think you ought to be. If you don't, why not? Will you commit today to repeating to yourself, "I deeply and completely accept myself, even when I am experiencing toxic shame. I deeply and completely accept myself, even when I don't do as well with _____ as I'd like." This will help you begin to accept yourself and where you're at in your journey, and not as you ought to be.

More importantly, I want to encourage you to commit to finishing this book no matter what. Don't let excuses, fear, or anything else get in your way. Healing is hard, and oftentimes, we try to talk ourselves out of it or justify why it can wait. Don't let this be you! Take the plunge into your healing journey TODAY. Fill in your signature and date below to make your commitment more tangible.

I, _____, commit to finishing this book, no matter what challenges come across my path during the days ahead. I know that I will most likely be faced with things that would try to get me off course and keep me from healing, but I'm choosing now to be proactive, to make my healing a priority and not let any excuses get in the way.

Sign here: _____

Date: _____

PART 1

WHAT IS TOXIC SHAME, AND HOW DO I KNOW IF I STRUGGLE WITH IT?

CHAPTER 2

DID YOU KNOW YOU MIGHT BE SUPERHUMAN?

I'm defective. I'm a mistake. I'm dirty. I'm ugly. I'm stupid. I'm not good enough. I am broken. I am worthless. What do all of these phrases have in common? They are all toxic self-assessments influenced by the negative comments from other people. They will tear you down, keep you paralyzed, and bind you in proverbial chains.

You can't do anything right. I can't believe how dumb you are. You're not smart enough. You're hopeless. Have you heard any of these phrases before? These are all toxically shaming phrases that people may have made in judgement of you.

Shame is a fruit of sin, and it is not a feeling God originally intended you to feel. How do I know this? Come with me to a story in Genesis 3. A long, long time ago, there was a woman named Eve. One day, she was out in the garden where she lived and a manipulative snake came to her and twisted God's words in order to entice her to ignore God's direction. She fell for the snake's trick and took a bite of fruit from the only tree God had told her not to eat from. Not only did she eat from it, she coaxed her husband to join her in rebellion as well. Immediately after partaking of the fruit, they realized they were naked and ran to put leaves together to cover themselves. Prior to this disobedience, there was no awareness that nakedness could be something shameful. In Genesis 2:25, it says, "And the man and his wife were both naked and were not ashamed." Can you imagine living in a world without clothes and there's no shame about it? I can't. But God, who can work *all* things for good, can use shame as an instrument for our good. He's amazing like that.

Shame is a feeling that acts as a signal. Your feelings act as yellow or red warning lights going off inside, telling you to pay attention and make a change, or to stop what you are doing altogether. On the flip side, they can be green lights, signaling to you that all is well. Each feeling we experience has a unique purpose. Shame's purpose is to signal human limitations. Once you recognize that shame is the emotion you're experiencing, you can then use that energy that shame is causing to set boundaries for yourself. I'll shed more light on this later in this book; just stick with me.

By now, you may be asking, "What is toxic shame exactly?" Brené Brown sums it up so well, unfortunately though, I don't remember where I came across this quote by her. She says shame is: "The intensely painful feeling or experience of believing that we are flawed and therefore, unworthy of love and belonging. 'I am bad.' 'I am a mess.' The focus is on the self, not behavior, and this often results in a feeling of loneliness. Toxic shame is never known to lead us toward positive change." If you allow toxic shame to control you, it will intertwine its viny arms all around the roots of your inner self, stifle you and keep you from flourishing. It will slowly take over, occupying more space and resources, slowly sucking the life out of everything around it.

If you allow the vine of shame to stick around, it will contaminate the way you see yourself and that can morph into toxic shame. Shame, similar to vines, can creep in almost anywhere and take a foothold.

Here's an illustration. The previous owners of our house planted vines in the fence line for privacy. These vines didn't just stay in the fence line, unfortunately. I continually found them creeping up in my flower bed, wrapping their tiny little fingers around my flowers. They even crept through cracks in our foundation, becoming almost impossible to pull out. They were persistent and didn't give up easily.

Toxic shame is the same way. It's a persistent little bugger, and can survive in almost any environment. When the vines are little, they are *much* easier to root out. However, if I don't check on my flowerbed for a while and let them grow, it's a much different story. They will intertwine their viny fingers all over my plants, and it will then become a huge task to get them out and find exactly where the root is.

The first time my husband and I went out and pulled up all of these vines and growth in the fence line, it took *all* day. It was *a lot* of work. It was messy and dirty. It wasn't fun or glamorous. Many times, I wanted to quit, and even wondered if the effort was worth it. But when we sat on our patio afterward and enjoyed the clean view, we both agreed it was indeed worth it.

Guess what? Next spring, the weeds returned! You can imagine my frustration. I didn't want to go through that *again*. But then again, I noticed that with each spring, there were fewer of them. Each season of uprooting unwanted vegetation got more of the deep roots. It was much easier, three or four growing seasons later, than it was the first time around!

Inner healing is a lot like uprooting the vines in our yard. It's messy. It takes time. It isn't fun. At different times, I wanted to quit pursuing my healing journey, but I remembered the end goal and kept going. Many times, I wondered if it was worth it. Honestly, sometimes, it got messier before it got better, which was unsettling. However, each and every time I persisted and I always advanced beyond that messy place. Thinking about the reward (healing and growth) on the other side always kept me going. The freedom and healing to be found made it all worth it. Slow and consistent progress ends up with big results.

I think it's important to note one thing here before moving on. The first time my husband and I went out to pull vines, we *thought* we got the root out, only to find that it sprang up again the next growing season. I thought it was going to be a "one and done" process for the most part; just a couple little stragglers to pull up here and there. It was disheartening and unexpected the next spring to see the fence covered again. Still, we went out and did the hard work again because we didn't want all of our work from the previous season to go to waste. I've experienced something similar in my healing journey.

At one point in my healing journey, I thought the worst was behind me, and from that point on, I'd just have to deal with a couple of straggling issues that would pop up here and there. But another season of life revealed a different story. Regardless of the temporary disappointments of revisiting old ground, I can say with absolute certainty that it's *always* been worth it to do the hard work of finding the root, digging it up and healing.

Toxic shame reflects on your being. It can cause you to either react as a superhuman, subhuman, or a combination of both. Let's take a look at each and see what they look like. When toxic shame is in superhuman form, it drives you to overcompensate with extraordinary performance and attempts at perfection.

A superhuman reaction makes you try to produce and perform at an unrealistic level in order to gain acceptance from those who would criticize you in the absence of perfection. Someone in superhuman mode always has to get an A in school. Top performance at work is a must. Saying *no* is difficult for such a person. This person thinks they are worthy because of what people say about them and what they accomplish. Average is not okay. This person feels that they must perform above average. A superhuman is more of a "human doing," not a "human being." Toxic shame driving a superhuman reaction is always about "doing something" to feel worthy.

A subhuman, on the other hand, goes to the polar extreme. Signs and symptoms of being subhuman are having thoughts such as, *I'm defective, I'm worthless, I'm a failure. People caught in subhuman shame* view themselves as less than other people. While a superhuman looks to the future, a subhuman tends to get stuck in the past. People stuck in this mode tend to isolate and withdraw. [1]

Do you identify with one of these? Personally, I have identified with both, and I'm not alone in this. You might be cruising along on the superhuman path for a while, but when a bump comes along - such as a criticism on a review at work - you resort to the subhuman track. You think you're a failure and you're worthless all because of one review that didn't meet "above average" standards.

---

1   Meier Clinic. Catalyst Program.

You might go into isolation and hide for a while. In my experience with this, I'd get tired of feeling subhuman, so I'd push myself to perform at a superhuman level again, in order to feel good about myself. Everything I did or didn't do defined me. I don't know about you, but I found this exhausting.

The good news is, there is another way! Just be *human!* As humans, we have needs. If I'm operating in the human category, then I need to be realistic about my needs and not always ignore them to satisfy other people's expectations. When I'm operating in the human category, fluctuating emotions are okay and normal. In fact, they are expected. Remember that emotions are signposts that tell us what's happening on the inside. Thus, we need to learn what those fluctuating feelings mean, and how to move forward with them in a healthy manner. The goal is to be human, to stay balanced, in the middle, and be fully human.

Here's a simple chart to summarize these ideas:

Superhuman	Performance, Perfection, Produce.	Human doing and not a human being. Often focused on the *future*.
Human	I have needs and I need to be realistic about them. Not always ignoring them to meet other people's expectations.	I'm human and I make mistakes. Stays in the *present*.
Subhuman	I'm defective. I'm a failure.	Tend to isolate and withdraw. Stuck in the *past*.

---

2 Meier Clinic. Catalyst Program Binder.

At this point, I imagine you might be wondering, if guilt and shame are the same thing? Good question! Actually, they are not the same. In the simplest of terms, guilt is, "I did something bad," while shame says, "I am bad." See the difference? One is focused on a behavior: "Oops, I messed up," "Something I did was not right, and it needs to be corrected." Whereas, shame is not a behavior, but rather, a belief: "*I am* bad at the core. I'm messed up. The problem is *me*. I should not even exist."

You should also know that there is something called false guilt and another thing called healthy shame. False guilt most commonly shows up when a decision is made that will most likely incur the disapproval of others. An example of this would be when all the teachers at your school stay for an optional event. And you, on the other hand, make the choice not to stay because of other considerations. For instance, you have a family at home that you haven't spent much time with, so you say "no" in order for you to stay with your family.

You may think that the other teachers - and even your boss - are judging you for your decision. This then creates an unpleasant, nagging sensation inside of you. You know you've made the best choice for you, but why doesn't it feel alright? That is false guilt.

As a side note, the more you work through false guilt and exercise rational decision-making, the less you will experience false guilt. Before moving onto the graph below, I also want to give you a brief description of healthy, as opposed to toxic, shame.

It's more like a feeling of modest embarrassment, but with compassion towards yourself. Let's say you give a speech and don't spend a lot of time preparing, and so, your performance reflects it. You are going to feel a level of embarrassment as people notice and react unfavorably. But with healthy shame, you are *not* beating yourself up, saying things like, "I'm a terrible speaker. I'm so stupid. I never should have done this." You are feeling a modicum of shame and rightfully so. It's embarrassing, but you take that embarrassment, learn from it, and do better next time. You say to yourself, "Okay, this was embarrassing, but I can step back, reassess and learn from this." "Next time, I won't say yes to a speaking engagement if I don't have the proper time to prepare." Healthy shame will give you energy to see what you did wrong, learn from it, and take a different direction next time.

Knowing there was such a thing as false guilt and healthy shame was a game-changer for me in my life! Below is a graph, breaking each down in concise, easy-to-remember terms.

TRUE GUILT *Violation of laws, rules, your values, or your beliefs. *Owning up to the fact that you messed up.	FALSE GUILT *Feeling guilty, meanwhile, you didn't do anything to violate your values, beliefs, or any law for that matter. *Lack of boundaries.
TOXIC SHAME * Declaring that you are a mistake, you're not worthy and you're broken.	HEALTHY SHAME * Admitting that you could have done better with more effort. * Signals human limitations.

[3]

Right now, you might be thinking, "Isn't what you're talking about normal, and something everyone experiences?" Well, I too, thought

---

3 Meier Clinic. Catalyst Program Binder.

my thinking about shame and guilt was *normal* until sometime in early adulthood, when God started showing me that the lies that I had believed were just that, and helped me see the truth.

I have learned in the past few years that children don't have the capacity to process things like adults, and so, they're unable to discern whether what they are being taught is true or not. If someone tells them something is true, they take it as true. This applies regardless of if children are being told about the world, or themselves.

Let me share an example of this from my own life. For me, a major insecurity was feeling unattractive. As a child, I don't remember hearing someone say that I was beautiful. The only thing I recall that was remotely flattering was my mom sharing something that my grandpa said. When I was a toddler, he told my parents that they had to watch out, or someone might kidnap me. It was his way of saying that I was really pretty.

However, outside of this, I can't recall any hints of being thought of as pretty. Of course, I know now that comparison is a dangerous place to go, but at the time, I didn't know how else to figure things out. So, I looked around me and compared myself to others my age. My observations told me that I was heavier than some of the other girls. My mom would make comments when I would gain or lose weight; I interpreted her observation as a criticism that I was too heavy. That probably wasn't her intended message, but that was the message I received.

Additionally, as I got a little older, I noted that other girls got noticed by boys… well, except for me. *I must not have been beautiful, if the boys didn't notice me, right?* On top of that, I didn't hear "you're beautiful" from other people, and I didn't see it myself. The first time I remember being called beautiful, I was in my early 20s. These experiences and my observations established what would become deep-rooted thinking in me for years to come: *I'm not beautiful.* Sadly, I took this as truth until my late 20s, which as I learned later, was not true at all.

For you, it may be that you never felt smart, important, or loved, but all of us experience insecurities at some point in our life. Sometimes, this is intentionally inflicted, but oftentimes, it's not. Irrespective of the intention, these unfortunate messages if left unchecked can cause toxic shame.

Going back to my vine analogy, shame has more than one thing in common with pesky, persistent vines. With both shame and vines, the longer they are allowed to grow and get a foothold, the longer it takes to find their roots and dig them out. If it didn't get there overnight, then it most likely won't come out overnight.

Overcoming the programming of the past may seem daunting, but I'll be here by your side, walking you through this journey until we find those roots and dig them out. In the next chapter, we'll be identifying our responses to shame. Together, you and me, hand in hand, will reach the other side, taking it one day at a time. It may get bumpy along the way, but trust me, it's worth it in the end. The freedom you will experience will be life-changing.

Action Steps—Jot down *all* of your thoughts today. Put them in two columns; the positive thoughts and negative thoughts. How do you talk to yourself? If more of your thoughts land on the negative side, the more likely it is that you struggle with toxic shame. My guess is that if you're reading this book, you already know you struggle with toxic shame. Admitting is the first step to healing. You can't overcome an issue that you refuse to acknowledge even exists. You're human. You make mistakes. That's okay. You are deeply and completely accepted by God as you are, and not as you believe that you ought to be.

CHAPTER 3

SYMPTOMS OF TOXIC SHAME

"Shame is among the most corrosive of human emotions, with the power to convince us that the little voice in our head is right after all — you know, the one that says, 'I knew you'd fail,' 'You'll never really belong,' and 'Who would love you?'".[1] David Sack, who is board certified in Psychiatry, Geriatric Psychiatry, and Addictive Psychiatry, makes a strong point in this excerpt from his article, and I am of the belief that he is right. We can't ignore shame. It will destroy us and turn toxic if we let it. It will keep us from our full potential and from truly living. Remember, toxic shame can be defined as the intensely painful feeling or experience of believing that we are so flawed that we are unworthy of acceptance and belonging. The impact of toxic shame on our lives is often ignored, overlooked, or pushed away. This often leads to it gaining a strong foothold and damaging our psyches in a number of ways. Shame can break up friendships and families, fuel addictions, trigger eating disorders, anxiety and even depression. It is so powerful that it can cause you to fail to live out your values and beliefs.

---

[1] "Recognizing the Red Flags of Shame – How Do You Feel?" Reach10. Last modified February 19, 2020. https://reach10.org/recognizing-red-flags-shame/.

This strong emotion triggers negative feelings about yourself that can be activated by even simple criticism or being challenged in the slightest. Things that can merely be embarrassing for a healthier person can morph into major life challenges for a person dealing with toxic shame.

In the course of my research for this book, I came across a diagram that perfectly and simply illustrates the various paths that shame can take. Please take a moment to look at the compass of shame below, and then I'll mention a few examples.

"Compass of Shame" designed by Donald Nathanson MD [2]

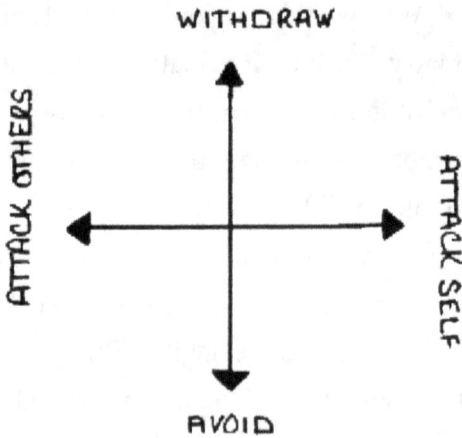

It is likely that you will be impacted by one of these compass points if you struggle with toxic shame.

---

2   Staff, IIRP. "4.5. Compass of Shame." IIRP Graduate School. Accessed December 11, 2021. https://www.iirp.edu/defining-restorative/compass-of-shame.

Let's examine these four responses, starting with **Attacking Others**. Imagine that you have a friend who is reacting to shame by acting out and verbally attacking other people, including you. This behavior will most likely stunt interpersonal relationships, whether or not the person being attacked withdraws from the relationship. Naturally, the relationship will not be *all* it could be. A relationship where one or both parties are attacking the other can be likened to a plant whose growth is stunted due to a lack of rain, fertilizer, sun, proper soil, etc. A plant, with all the components for necessary and proper care will grow and flourish. The same is true with friendships. If both parties in the relationship are providing the necessary nutrients, the relationship will blossom and develop in a healthy way.

Here is an example of this compass point:

I have a friend that I'll call Andrea. Because of her parents' tendency to verbally lash out at her and her siblings, and an apparent need to incessantly blame others, my friend Andrea completely cut off all ties with them. This had been a pattern throughout her life, and her parents' denial kept them from seeing their part in the estrangement. The damage they were *still* causing their children as adults was so extreme that she felt she had to remove them from her life. The impact of the pattern of criticism and blame made the relationship itself toxic. In most cases, a complete loss of contact with the person perpetrating the attacks will not be necessary. However, being in relationship (family, friendship or romantic) with someone who is constantly and repeatedly attacking you will obviously keep that relationship from growing and flourishing.

Now, let's continue our way around the compass to **Withdraw**. Sometimes I like to look up synonyms to give me more clarity. Synonyms for this withdraw include: depart, disengage, leave, pull back, or quit. Withdrawal can be emotional, physical, or both.

Withdrawal was my response to my husband accidentally triggering old shame wounds from my childhood. Shortly after we were married, when my husband, a man I adore and has more positive qualities than negative, invalidated my feelings or if I sensed a conflict coming on, I'd immediately withdraw emotionally, and sometimes, even physically; for instance, I'd often pull my hand away from his. I had spent many years being invalidated by family, and even though I *knew* in my head that my husband did not mean to trigger me, once my heart detached emotionally, I didn't know how to recover in that moment. Over the course of our marriage, as I've continued with my healing, my tendency to withdraw emotionally has become non-existent.

The third point of the compass is **Attacking Self**. Another way to look at it is being *unduly hard on yourself*. This is reflected in thinking like: *I'm stupid. I am a failure at my job. I'm a horrible mom. I'm ugly. I'm fat.*

My friend, Miriam[3] experienced toxic shame in her work environment when technology was involved. In her early years of teaching, the use of technology was minimal and learning more about it was not something that she focused on. As technology became more prevalent in the classroom, she found that most of her co-workers were better with technology than her, which led to her feeling

---

3   Used with permission

inadequate and triggered feelings of toxic shame. She was hard on herself by saying things like: *I'm so dumb. What's wrong with ME?*

She was harsher on herself than she would have been with a fellow teacher in the same situation. A litmus test to use when attacking yourself is to ask: *Would I say this to someone else? Is it kind? Would I talk to my child this way?*

Finally, there's **Avoidance**. Avoidance leads to you denying that toxic shame even exists in your life. Someone living with avoidance of their shame may distract themselves through thrill-seeking or numbing via drugs and alcohol or other distractions. Avoidance keeps you from feeling the extent of your pain in some form or fashion. You may also avoid certain people or situations who trigger your shame.

My friend, Sharron shared a tangible example of this from her life. She suffered from a medical condition that caused excessive sweating, and it became a source of insecurity, extreme embarrassment and eventually, toxic shame. She was careful in how she dressed and even the pencils she wrote with, in order to try to minimize the possibility of her excess sweating becoming discovered or more prominent.

When she was in college, a kind and godly young man showed interest in her. She felt unworthy of his attention and found herself ignoring his phone calls at first, and eventually, cutting off all communication with him. She never told him why she feigned disinterest. Avoiding having people discover her medical condition was a driving force in her life.

Now, maybe she wouldn't have ended up marrying the nice classmate even if she had dated him, but I think you can see just how much this decision might have completely altered the course of her life.

The first stop on our journey to dealing with toxic shame is to *admit* that we struggle with it; without admitting it, we can't work on it. I believe that the reason you are reading this book though is because you've already admitted it, right? As we go through this chapter, we'll see how toxic shame affects us physically, through our thoughts and behaviors. As someone who has walked through this journey, I can promise you, it's worth it to expose and heal the effects of toxic shame. Once you learn that you, God and others, love you deeply, then you'll be able to begin accepting yourself just as you are.

It might be hard to believe that you can completely accept yourself. For many years, I didn't fully accept myself either. I tried to get rid of or hide what I considered the ugly parts of me. For example, I didn't accept being an introvert, or that I was having trouble finding the right words in uncomfortable conversations or those that I felt were unsafe. I didn't like the way my tone changed when I felt unsafe, my super-strong need for self-protection, the sound of my voice or laugh, and similar personal traits. Completely accepting myself was an alien concept for me, until a few years ago, when my counselor opened my eyes to this; I understand that it may still be strange for you, and I'm here to walk through this process with you. I resisted at first, like you very well may be doing now. I also want you to know, it's okay to not have the zeal or desire to begin. It's a process, just stick with it.

The way my counselor explained it to me was that all facets of our personality are needed. Some work very hard to protect us, and that's their job! The goal of this journey is to heal the parts of our personality that are out of proportion, so that they do not dominate and control us. Imagine yourself wearing medieval armor. How convenient will it be for you to move around? Not very convenient, right? It will affect your everyday life. Toxic shame is like that, affecting your everyday life, slowing you down and hindering you from being able to fully function.

I want to give an example of what I'm talking about before proceeding. Let's take a look at self-protection. The instinct for self-protection is triggered when fear threatens our basic needs and tells us to fight or flee. If a bad guy is approaching, we need to be able to protect ourselves by running away or physically confronting him so we can get away. By default, you protect yourself from danger. God gave us the ability to recognize and react when danger is present. Now, let's look at this in an emotional sense. If someone attacks you verbally, if you feel safe, you will be able to speak up and express that you don't like it; you can also ask them not to talk to you in that manner anymore. If your sense of self-protection is too easily triggered, you might become aggressive (fight), or freeze up and go quiet (flee).

By now, I hope you are seeing the urgency of waking up to toxic shame and ridding yourself of it. If you're like me, you like practical, tangible help, not something too vague or hard to understand. So, if you're asking, "How can I recognize toxic shame? What are the signs that I struggle with it? What does it feel like?" you're in luck. We are going to go into detail about the physical symptoms of toxic shame and how it shows up in our thoughts and behaviors.

First, let's talk about physical symptoms. You already know that our bodies give us signals when something is not right physically. It's our body's way of letting us know something needs to be dealt with, and for us to stop and take a look at it. The body does the same thing with situations that negatively impact us. Until a few years back, I didn't realize how much information my body gave me. I thought that tightness in the chest when nervous was something everyone experienced. I thought everyone's breathing slowed down when they were nervous. I didn't know my body was telling me that I needed to stop and take a look at what was causing those reactions. Our bodies remember traumas from the past, even if we don't consciously remember them. These stored memories or trauma can trigger reactions in our body when we experience a similar event. However, not all of our reactions are due to past memories or trauma. But our bodies do *talk* to us and communicate a lot of valuable information; we only need to slow down, observe and listen.

HOW SHAME SHOWS UP IN THE BODY [4]

- ☐ You may feel a *pull* to look down and avoid eye contact.
- ☐ Your shoulders may slump.
- ☐ You may feel tightness in your chest.
- ☐ Your face may feel hot or even turn red.
- ☐ You may feel discomfort in your stomach.
- ☐ Your body or your words may *feel* frozen.
- ☐ You may feel a sense of defeat.

---

[4] Meier Clinic. Catalyst Binder.

- ☐ You may want to curl up in a fetal position or stay in bed all day.
- ☐ You may experience the urge to be alone and hide.

The compass of shame gave us an overview of shame's primary patterns of response. Now, it's time to get up close and more specific with the symptoms that you may be experiencing, and which lead to a diagnosis of toxic shame.

SYMPTOMS OF TOXIC SHAME[5]

- Paralysis - What comes to mind when you hear the word paralysis? It's probably someone who is unable to move their entire body, or a part of their body. We primarily think of it in a physical way. Do you know that shame can paralyze you emotionally? If your toxic shame is being triggered by someone else's words or behavior, you might want to say something to "defend" yourself, but you may not find the right words. Your words might be frozen in your mind, and you find yourself unable to speak them. You may want to be able to run away, but feel physically immobilized.

    The paralysis could be emotional, physical or both. Personally, it shows up with my words being "frozen" when I feel like I am under attack. The more I heal, the less this happens, but it still shows up on occasion. Paralysis can compound the shame you are feeling, because there's a good chance you are criticizing yourself for not being strong enough to stand up for yourself or being too afraid to walk away.

---

[5] Meier Clinic. Catalyst Binder.

- Faltering energy - Not only does shame steal self-worth, it also can suck the energy and life out of you. Emotions take energy, and so does tearing yourself down with negative thinking. Most people feel small and weak in the face of a shaming attack. Living with toxic shame and toxic thinking is exhausting.
- Escapism - We humans don't like to experience pain; either on a physical or emotional level. Before I had the tools to cope with the emotional pain toxic shame caused me, one escape for me was to binge-eat. Despite that it provided temporary relief, I knew that in the end, I'd feel worse, but I did it anyway. Other people turn to drugs, sex or alcohol to numb the pain. Others may always keep themselves busy with friends or work, so that they don't have any quiet time to think about their lives. Some stay up late binging on a favorite television program so they don't feel alone when it gets quiet at night, and it is time to go to bed. Others may develop a gambling problem. None of these escape routes is a cure for the pain of toxic shame; they are only Band-Aids or temporary fixes
- Withdrawal – This symptom is so common that it is one of the compass points! This is the symptom that I struggled with the longest. When I was struggling with binge-eating, it would lead to withdrawal in a physical sense. I would avoid people at work whenever possible, and after work, I would just stay home by myself. I was afraid people would ask personal questions, and my elaborately covered toxic shame would be exposed. I believed people would despise me if they saw my true self. Hiding your true self might take on the appearance

of people-pleasing, always smiling, having the need to say something in every conversation, or appearing confident and in control. In reality, it is a cover for withdrawal from uncomfortable situations.

- Perfectionism - Another way people try to hide their shame is by trying to do everything perfectly. People convince themselves that toxic shame will just go away if they do everything perfectly and not make any mistakes. Oftentimes, a person hiding behind perfectionism will not even attempt something, if they can't do it well. Of all the toxic shame symptoms, I believe this one is more exhausting than all of the others. I mean, trying to be perfect *all* the time? I get tired just at the mere thought of it. There is so much freedom to be found in realizing that you are *human,* and humans make mistakes. Toxic shame makes this hard to believe.
- Criticism & blame - People suffering from toxic shame can become highly critical of others. By pointing out the weaknesses of others, they feel better about themselves and thus, convince themselves that they are superior to others. They may also blame other people for their problems to avoid taking responsibility for their behavior. The combination of being critical and blaming others helps keep their shame hidden. This symptom is one that can be *incredibly* damaging for the people on the receiving end of the criticism and blame.
- Rage - Rage is violent or uncontrollable anger due to a perceived slight or other triggering event. More subtle forms of anger can either be justifiable, or a mere overreaction. Many times, a person's outburst of rage often surprises or confuses

onlookers, and they are left wondering what just happened. If a person suffering from toxic shame believes they are being attacked, and their shame is about to be exposed, they may overcompensate with excessive anger in an attempt to keep their shame hidden. People who exhibit rage are often seen as unreasonable, because they can become furious over the slightest thing. Those whose reaction to shame is rage may become verbally or physically abusive. Rage is used to protect their sense of self-worth.

- Denial—Denial is a defense mechanism against shame. Persistent denial involves self-delusion, and this can make a person unaware of the continued presence of toxic shame. People desire to be accepted by others, and may deliberately blind themselves to what would bring feelings of shame, so they pretend it doesn't exist.
- Exhibitionism - This symptom of shame attempts to mask pain by flamboyant behavior or dress. Exhibitionists may appear confident, but in reality, they use clothing, sexuality, or attention-seeking to divert attention from their inner shame.
- Self-sabotage - Self-sabotage is a result of a lack of self-esteem. It stems from feelings of anxiety or worthlessness, due to toxic shame. These people blame themselves for everything, and are cruel and harsh judges of their own behavior and thinking. When they share their harsh assessments of themselves with others, they may seek external validation and approval. Self-sabotage can take many forms, but I wanted to give you a brief glimpse of what it could look like. If you think this might be

you, I encourage you to do some more research and see how it shows up in your life.

The above list gives a bird's eye view of toxic shame and how to recognize it. Now I'm going to get into the nitty gritty and talk about how it might show up specifically in various thoughts and behaviors. I'll go through a series of questions and provide examples of each so hopefully you can begin to have more clarity and see if any of them resonate with you.

HOW SHAME SHOWS UP IN THOUGHTS & BEHAVIORS

- Do you have a fear of abandonment?

    For the longest time, I thought I didn't. But in the past few years, I've come to realize I did, but in less obvious ways. I wasn't afraid of my friends leaving me, neither did I have thoughts of my parents walking away from me and never seeing them again, so I thought I didn't struggle with abandonment. I did fear however, without even knowing it, that people might abandon me by rejecting me emotionally. So, as it turns out, I did struggle with abandonment — emotional abandonment. I believed that I was *bad* in my personality; that something was *wrong* with *me*. I always thought I didn't belong in my family; it started from small things like the fact that everyone liked nuts and shrimp in my family but me, to bigger things like my personality. In my teenage years, things were getting bumpy with my parents. I noticed my brothers seemed to avoid these bumps and run ins. This, among other things, led me to believe there was something wrong with *me* and my personality. I believed I was defective, that I was a mistake, that I was broken.

- Do you become like a chameleon hiding in the garden?

    If you struggle with shame and fear of rejection, you might be like the chameleon, blending in with his surroundings. You become what you believe everyone around you wants you to be. In simple terms, you become a people-pleaser.

- Do you put everyone else's needs (physically, emotionally, and spiritually) above your own? Do you consistently neglect yourself for the benefit of others, until you are run down and empty? Do you exhaust all parts of yourself until you are barely crawling, but still don't stop to take care of yourself?

    Make no mistake, I'm not against trying to meet the needs of others out of love. Sometimes, we do need to make sacrifices. What I am referring to is *always* meeting everyone else's needs *at the detriment of your* own needs. This is unhealthy because it causes you to be run down, with nothing left to offer anyone.

- Do you undermine your chances of success or happiness, thinking you don't deserve them? Do you self-sabotage and work *against* yourself instead of *for* yourself?

    Self-sabotage can show up as perfectionism; i.e., you don't do something at all if you think you can't do it perfectly. It may show up as low self-worth, meaning you see your dream job, but don't apply because your low self-worth says to you, *you won't get it anyway.* Your internalized shame won't allow you to succeed. If you hear yourself saying, "I shot myself in the foot," you very well may be self-sabotaging in that moment.

- Do you find yourself humiliating others, so you don't get humiliated?

    Shame is a threat to your sense of well-being. Shame leaves you feeling exposed and vulnerable. In order to avoid this, you may pass the shame onto someone else so your ego can be left intact and so you can avoid those intolerable feelings of deep-rooted shame.

- Do you have addictive behaviors?

    Shame and addiction go hand in hand. The more you have been shamed, the more likely you are to exhibit addictive behaviors. The pain will seem almost unbearable, so, anything that promises relief from the pain and internal emptiness will look appealing. Addictions can show up in many forms. Here are some of the common ones: alcohol, drugs, sex, food, work, another person, shopping, gambling, always needing to have a relationship, etc. This is by no means an exhaustive list.

It's important to note here that just because someone you know struggles with one of the above symptoms, doesn't mean it is due to toxic shame. Avoid diagnosing other people as having toxic shame. Use this information as a tool to help *you* see if you need to heal from toxic shame, rather than diagnose others around you.

Facing pain and admitting we struggle with shame can be difficult, and even scary. You may be thinking, "But I've been like this my whole life. This is just the way I am." Or, "I've been this way so long; it's too late to change." I want to encourage you that it's *never* too late! While you may be correct that you cannot do it on your own, God can help you. God is the God of what we consider to be impossible. He is a healer and restorer of things we never thought could be fixed.

Up until 50 years ago, most people thought the human brain and resulting thought processes were programmed to be a "certain way" and thus, were unchangeable. If you had a limitation for whatever reason, you were just taught how to cope and live with it. Now, researchers and doctors are learning that the brain is malleable. They have proven that YOU can reconceptualize toxic thoughts. YOU can tell yourself a new story. YOU can rewrite your ending. YOU are not stuck where you are currently, just because your family of origin or biology predisposed you that way.

A term that I'm hearing about a lot, in both books and podcasts, is "neuroplasticity." According to the Oxford Languages Dictionary, neuroplasticity is "the ability of the brain to form and reorganize synaptic connections, especially in response to learning or experience or following injury." [6]

Dr. Caroline Leaf, a researcher and cognitive (mind) neuroscientist, who has done lots of research on the brain talks about in her podcasts how avoiding or suppressing a feeling or emotion only makes it stronger and more intense. I don't know about you, but shame isn't a feeling that I want intensified! It is encouraging to learn that the human brain is adaptable, and that God can lead us to healing. So, even though it's scary at times and it may be a bumpy road, I encourage you to take the journey, face your shame, process it, and heal from it.

---

6   "NEUROPLASTICITY English Definition and Meaning | Lexico.com." Lexico Dictionaries | English. Accessed December 11, 2021. https://www.lexico.com/en/definition/neuroplasticity.

I know that I just gave you a lot of information. Don't worry. We're going to take some time at the end of this chapter to reflect and have an honest conversation with ourselves. You're probably scared right now; you're considering closing the book and running away. That's okay. Dr. Caroline Leaf, often talks about learning to be *okay* with the uncomfortable. When I first heard this concept, it was foreign to me. I don't like emotional discomfort. It's something I used to do almost anything to avoid. It triggered toxic thinking for me of *This will last forever*, which took me back to a painful and scary place; a place I would do almost anything to avoid. But I have since learned to accept and try to embrace the uncomfortable. Dr. Caroline Leaf also says in her 21 Day Brain Detox how feelings are like a wave; they will pass. They don't last forever. I encourage you to deeply and completely accept yourself and where you are at right now. Try to accept and sit with these uncomfortable feelings as we wrap up this chapter. The uncomfortable feelings will pass. They are just waves, passing through. You won't be stuck here forever, if you don't want to be. You have more control than you think you do right now. You are loved, right where you are by the Creator of the Universe and me. Take that thought with you now as we conclude this chapter.

It's important to note that many of these symptoms discussed in this chapter could be similar to those of other 'sin diseases.' Just like when you have a cold, your nose might get stuffy, and as a result, you temporarily lose your sense of smell. This same thing can also be a symptom of covid-19. Just because you lose your sense of smell doesn't mean you have covid-19. Further examining and testing needs to be done to confirm. Therefore, just because you have one of the symptoms of shame doesn't mean you have deep-rooted shame either. You have to look at all the symptoms, be honest with yourself, and do some further examining. However, remember, shame is a feeling. All of us experience shame at various times in our life, just like any other emotion. Shame can actually be healthy or unhealthy. Healthy shame signals that we are outside of our human limitations and need to use that energy to set boundaries. It's the undealt-with shame that gets toxic, causes problems, and tears us down; this is unhealthy.

    I want to add another real-life example, used with permission, from my friend Sharron. When she was three years old, she was arguing with her brothers in the backseat of the car over something she wanted. She recalls saying something like, *I want that. I want that.* Her dad called out to the back seat, saying something along the lines of, *You need to shut up.* She didn't, and it wasn't long before her dad asked her, "*Do you want me to put you outside the car?*" Her three-year-old self retorted, "*Yeah, I do.*" Dad said, "*Okay,*" and next thing she knew, she was left alone on the side of the highway, terrified. In that moment, she decided she was *never* going to speak up again. She *lost* her voice, changing her life from that point forward. No one spoke up for her, and she interpreted that to mean that she wasn't worthy. Her self-talk became *I'm not acceptable. I shouldn't speak up or I will be abandoned. I deserve to be by myself. I don't make wise decisions. I'm not smart.* At the age of three, Sharron didn't have the ability to process that on her own, and so, the shame stayed with her for the next forty-something years and became toxic. It kept her from living her full potential and truly living. Praise Jesus that in the past few years, God helped her start breaking free from that toxic shame, find her voice, and truly start to live. However, before that healing could happen in her life, she had to admit and recognize shame as part of her story.

To wrap up this chapter, I want to refresh your memory, on what toxic thinking - also known as negative inner dialogue or self-talk - sounds like. Unhealthy shame says, *"I'm defective. I'm a mistake. I'm dirty. I'm ugly. I'm stupid. I'm not good enough. I am broken. I am worthless. I can't do anything right. I can't believe how dumb I am. I am not smart enough. I am hopeless."* These are the thoughts and inner dialogue that you need to take seriously. They are NOT harmless! They are lies and they need to be changed to truth. Tell yourself a new story! Starting now! It will take work, and it won't happen overnight, but I promise you, IT WILL BE WORTH IT. Later on, we'll go deeper into what positive self-talk or inner self dialogue looks like, but for now, let's keep it simple and start making baby changes TODAY. Going forward, start paying attention to your thoughts and how you talk to yourself. When you catch yourself saying something similar to the ones in italics above, please stop what you're doing, replace that thought with truth and tell yourself, "It's okay. I'm human and I make mistakes. I deeply and completely accept myself, even when I struggle with toxic thinking." You got this! I believe in YOU!

Action Steps—Find some place quiet and safe. Turn on relaxing music and breathe in and out slowly. Do this until you feel the tightness in your chest leave, or your heart rate go down. When you feel relaxed and at ease, re-read, "HOW SHAME SHOWS UP IN THE BODY", "SYMPTOMS OF SHAME "and "HOW SHAME SHOWS UP IN THOUGHTS & BEHAVIORS." Give yourself permission to admit the places in your life where shame is showing up. Face your fear so you can begin to heal. Place checkmarks in the boxes that you identify and resonate with. Put an 'x' in the box of those you don't see at all in your life. Please, please, please, take an honest and hard look at yourself. It's okay. Allow yourself to be human. Humans make mistakes. Evaluate where you are right now, so that you can begin taking the journey toward healing. Remember, admitting the ways in which you struggle is the first step forward!

Never forget, you are deeply and completely accepted, even when you struggle with unhealthy shame. Stick with me, and in the next chapter, we'll look at where shame originates from.

Bonus Action Step: Another way to do this is to close your eyes and listen to your body. Breathe in and out slowly, while focusing on your breath. Now, imagine yourself in a situation where shame is being triggered. What does your body feel? What are you doing with your head? Does your face feel warm? Do you feel the urge to hide? What thoughts or inner dialogue is happening inside your mind at this moment? Are you being kind and gentle to yourself or hard on yourself? Would you speak this way to a friend? Remember, we want to start becoming aware of our thoughts and inner dialogue so that we can begin to tell ourselves a new story.

PART 2

WHERE DOES TOXIC SHAME COME FROM?

CHAPTER 4

THE ORIGINS OF SHAME

"How we think not only affects our own spirit, soul, and body, but also, people around us. Science and Scripture both show how the results of our decisions pass through the sperm and ova to the next four generations, profoundly affecting their choices and lifestyles. The science of epigenetics (the signals, including our thoughts, that affects the activity of our genes) explains how this plays out. This reminds me of the Scripture, 'he punishes the children and their children for the sin of the parents to the third and fourth generation (Exodus 34:7).'" [1]

Before reading this in her book, "Switch on Your Brain," I never understood that passage of scripture. It didn't seem to match the character of the God I see in the Bible to punish grandchildren for something their great grandfather did. I left it up to one of those scriptures I may never fully understand, but trusted God to make it clear one day. Eventually, I was able to make sense of it when I read what Dr. Caroline Leaf said. In the last couple years, I've been learning how much our thinking can affect our brain and its health. Our thinking can change our DNA! Can you believe that? I don't have time to go into all of it here, and I'm no expert on the matter, but if this

---

1   Leaf, Caroline. Switch On Your Brain: The Key to Peak Happiness, Thinking, and Health. Ada: Baker Books, 2013: pg 24

interests you, I encourage you to check out the book, "Switch on Your Brain." Dr. Caroline Leaf has done decades of research on the brain, and personally, I find it fascinating. It has been blowing my mind!

Wait, so you're saying my family is to blame for my shame? That it's passed down to me because the thinking patterns of my ancestors - which didn't change from generations ago - affected their DNA and now, mine is inevitably affected? The answer to those questions isn't a simple yes or no, so, please allow me to explain further. My point here is, there are things passed down from generation to generation; some of it through DNA, and some of it through generational patterns that have not been broken. This implies that they're being passed on from one generation to the next, until someone in the family breaks them. But as Dr. Caroline Leaf loves to say, "You are not a victim of your biology!" We can't control the event and circumstances of our life, but we can control how we respond to them. And as we do so, we can change the brain and its pathways to new, healthier ones. You don't have to stay stuck in the cycles you have found yourself in for years or maybe even decades. I won't lie to you and say it's easy; it definitely takes work, but eventually, the fruit of your labor will be worth it! As we'll learn in the next chapter, it can dramatically change our relationships, and cause us to be better friends, spouses, employees… you name it.

There's a good chance that a lot of your toxic shame and thinking is from your family of origin. Our families have the greatest influence on our lives. The most influential years are the first two years. Things you may not even remember may be impacting you today. Crazy, right? Our bodies store those memories. Toxic shame doesn't always come from childhood; however, I think it's safe to say that for the most part, the toxic shame and thinking you are currently dealing with most likely stemmed from your younger days. It could be from something traumatic or something minor that you'd never have considered was of that much importance to impact you, until you dig deeper.

Personally, I know most, if not all of my toxic shame and stinkin 'thinkin' (toxic thinking/lies) are a direct result of the kind of childhood I experienced. I know I'm not alone in this because as we learned in chapter 2, children on their own don't possess the skillset to process thoughts and messages like, *I'm not good enough, there's something wrong with me, I'm broken, I can't do anything right, I'm a failure, and I'm defective.* I didn't know any better at the time, and neither did you. So, please don't be hard on yourself. I imagine you - like me - did the best you could at the time. My observations, like yours, told me they were true, so I took them as truth. As a result, we just took those thoughts and messages we received as truth and didn't question them. We didn't have people around us to help us process and work through them. Or, you probably kept quiet because of toxic shame, so you wouldn't be exposed.

The toxic thoughts and shame that plague you today as an adult may have come from incidents on the playground as a kid, a bully at school, the neighbor's kid, or simply an offhand comment from someone—a teacher, parent, or sibling. Unhealthy thinking can be triggered by something we heard either directly or indirectly (overt and covert), things taken personally that were not personal at all, or messages that you misinterpreted and internalized. For many of us, our toxic shame has its roots in our family of origin. It could look like a parent never admitting they messed up which can send a shaming message to kids. Love based on performance can also grow toxic shame in a child. Parental perfectionism, abandonment (emotionally or physically), abuse (physical, emotional, verbal, sexual), deficiency messages, or being forced to keep the family "secrets." Remember, shame can grow in many places and take many forms. This is just a few examples to give you an idea of how toxic shame often begins.

There are two different types of shaming—covert and overt. To explain this more clearly, I'll share another story of my friend, Miriam. Miriam started struggling with bouts of depression from the young age of nine. When she looked around her, no one else was struggling with it. No one got her. She felt so alone. In the environment she was in, depression wasn't even considered a real thing. Can you see how this could cause shame over struggling with depression? To make matters worse, people even called her Crazy Miri. Can you imagine? My heart breaks for her just thinking about what this must have been like. Her story shows examples of both covert and overt shaming.

The overt shaming is easier to recognize (Crazy Miri), and the covert (denying depression is even a real thing), is more subtle. The latter is harder to recognize, but that doesn't mean it has less of an impact. In fact, covert shaming, like emotional trauma, can mess with your head even more. Why's that, you may ask? Because it's harder to prove. It often gets overlooked, dismissed, or minimized. It isn't talked about as much, leaving the individual experiencing it to question and second-guess everything happening to them. Dear reader, I want you to know that I hear you and I see you. You are not crazy. You desire to be heard and I hear you. Not only do I hear you, but your Heavenly

Daddy who loves you so much wants to bring you healing if you'll let Him. How do I know this? Because I've seen it firsthand, over the last few years for myself in my own life.

If you don't know this Heavenly Daddy that I'm talking about, please allow me to tell you about Him now. He's crazy about YOU! He loves you more than you can ever imagine! He loves you so much He sent His only Son, Jesus, to come die on the cross for the sins you and I commit against him. He did this knowing how much we would sin against Him and hurt Him. But His love was so great that He paid that high price to get us back, so we would have a relationship with Him again. See, our sin created a great gap between us, and He desired to close that gap. He loves YOU and wants a relationship with YOU! I know, it sounds too good to be true, right? This is love like we've never known. But I'm here to tell you His love is real, deep, and genuine. He DELIGHTS in you! Did you know that? How many people in your life have delighted in YOU? This was transformational for me. I didn't know anyone truly delighted in me and accepted me as I was and not as I ought to be for a big part of my life. And the best part about all this is…IT'S FREE! You don't have to pay money to get this kind of love. You don't have to earn it. All you have to do is believe in the Lord Jesus Christ and YOU WILL BE SAVED! The wages of your sin were death (Romans 6:23). But God sent his Son to pay that price by dying on the cross to cover that debt. If we accept His gift, we are given ETERNAL LIFE. This isn't about religion. It's about a life-changing, transformational relationship with the one who created you and knows you better than you know yourself. [2]

---

2 For more information: "Why Is Salvation Through Christ Alone?" Crosswalk.com. Last modified February 1, 2021. https://www.crosswalk.com/faith/spiritual-life/why-is-salvation-through-christ-alone.html.

Now, let's get back to covert and overt shaming. Let's go with an example that I imagine all of us can relate to — grades in school. An example of overt shaming could be a parent upon seeing a report card of 3 A's and 1 B saying to a child, "What's wrong with you? You can do better! Why didn't you get all A's like your sister?" Now, let's use this same example to see what overt shaming might look like. This same example of a parent looking at a report card and seeing 3 A's and 1 B might say something like this, "When I was in school, I never settled for anything less than all A's. You're going to have to work harder than this."

Some families are experts in shaming, and thus, throw it back and forth to each other all the time, like a downpour of rain, affecting everything in the *garden*. Other families may target only one or two family members, making them the family scapegoat. The family scapegoat often carries their shame with them into adulthood, always expecting to be shamed, criticized, blamed and diminished. It's a painful place to be.

Right now, you might be overwhelmed. Wanting to put in the work, but too tired and afraid to do so. The dark hole you find yourself in may lead you to think you are doomed. Dear friend, you are NOT doomed. I know you're tired. I hear you. I feel you. I see you. Hold on to hope, love. One small step forward with consistency will lead to big changes. Let's just take it one moment at a time, one thought at a time, one day at a time, and one day, you'll be running again. You are not in this alone. I am here with you; there are also others on this journey with you. If you want, you can join my author Facebook page (Emily Ehe-Author) and find support amongst others. I will jump in when I can with support and encouragement. We are not meant to do this alone! We need friends to carry us along with their support and encouragement when we are weak. If you have learned nothing else from this chapter, I hope you've learned that THERE IS HOPE! Your past does *not* have to dictate your future. You can't control what happens *to* you all the time, but you can always control your response to what happens to you. Let's start taking control of what we can control.

Action Steps—Get away to some place quiet. Turn on relaxing and calming music. Breathe in and out with it until you are in a relaxed state. Ask God to show you where shame is coming for you personally. Ask Him to show you when you felt shame for the first time. Ask Him to show you where He was when this event was taking place. Ask him to show you the truth. I reckon that this may be new for you, as I was once at this point myself. Give yourself grace as you practice listening to God. The more you do it, the better you will become. It's a skill like anything else. During your time of listening, try not to overthink it. Afterwards, I encourage you to find someone *safe* to process it with; preferably someone who knows scripture and can point you to the truth of who God says you are. This is highly advised because, whenever we sit and listen to God, it's always a good idea to take it back to the Bible to see if what we think we heard from God matches up with what He says in scripture. If it doesn't match up with the Bible, then it's not from Him. [3]

---

3 Rustenbach, Rusty. *A Guide for Listening and Inner-Healing Prayer:* Meeting God in the Broken Places. Carol Stream: Tyndale House, 2014.

PART 3

WHY YOU CAN'T IGNORE IT ANY LONGER

CHAPTER 5

THE FRUIT OF TOXIC SHAME

"What we don't need in the midst of struggle is shame for being human."

~Brené Brown

Have you ever been shamed for being human? I know I have. I have been shamed for having emotions, when in reality, having emotions is part of being human. Now, while we CANNOT let emotions control us, we should not ignore them either, as emotions are signals, telling us what is happening inside of us. I have been shamed while processing emotions with people; this is scary for someone who used to be closed off and had to learn to open up to safe people. I have been shamed for dating cross-culturally. I have been shamed in the workplace, in my marriage, and believe it or not, even in the church. Shame literally shows up everywhere: the family, church, work, playground, neighborhoods, marriages... the list is endless. Shame will show up anywhere there's a crack that will allow it in. We can all relate to this, as we've all been shamed at some point in our lives.

The truth of the matter is, we're all humans, and as humans, we make mistakes. Ever since sin entered the world with Adam and Eve, it's been an inevitable part of life. I don't think a lot of times people even realize they are shaming others. This doesn't excuse what they are doing, but it's helpful for me to know that people don't generally do it on purpose. Oftentimes, it's an automatic response coming from a wound that hasn't been healed. The good news is, we have a choice to not give in to shaming others as result of our own wounding! We can choose to put in the work to heal that wound, or continue on the way we are.

Personally, that choice was easy to make. The fruits of healing and dealing with shame far outweigh the cost. Living a life where shame had its viny little fingers all over was a miserable way to live, in my experience. True life wasn't happening there. It's probable that you find yourself just going through the motions of life. Do you really enjoy that? I know I didn't. As a young adult, sometimes I'd find myself thinking, "If this is all life has to offer, then let me just die now. A whole lifetime of *this* just doesn't sound fun to me. Work, sleep, work, sleep, with problems along the way now and then." I didn't see the purpose in it. Another 50 years or more of it sounded awful to me. But the more God brought healing to the various parts of me that got wounded through this journey called life, the more I began too truly live. When I finally dealt with my shame, WOW!! MY WHOLE WORLD WAS FILLED WITH COLOR!! I began to finally be me and revel in who God intended me to be! I felt FREE and it was beautiful!!

Can you believe my shame kept me from laughing out loud?! Now, I find myself laughing out loud while watching something funny on TV or when my husband says something funny. In the past, my shame kept me from dancing around the house when something would excite me. Now, when I make a sale on a book, or Emily Rae Creations (a small business that I started), I start dancing up and down like a little kid in the Christmas spirit. Stinkin' thinkin' (toxic thinking) kept me from learning how to draw and getting into photography. Fast forward to this present moment, I get so much joy from painting and taking pictures. And it doesn't stop there; now, I even sell painted postcards. As much as these new activities were a big deal for me, what excited me the most was that I eventually became brave enough to put myself out there to possibly be embarrassed. Shame kept me from playing sports because I believed I wasn't good and I wanted to avoid embarrassment. But looking back, I think I wasn't good because I never practiced, as, not too many people start out good. Remember how shame can keep us from doing stuff when we aren't good at it. That was me. I think I would have been good if I hadn't just quit right off the bat. Perhaps I would have enjoyed playing softball, volleyball, or even track.

What area of your life do you think shame has held you back in? Did it keep you from your dream job? Does it keep you from being the kind of parent you want to be? Does it keep you from being vulnerable in friendships? Maybe it even has such a tight grip on you, it keeps you locked safely inside your house?

Shame is sneaky and quiet, hiding and lurking in the secret corners of your garden. Don't let it deceive or blind you. You only have one life to live, so, why not make it count and live it to the fullest? If you aren't fully convinced how necessary it is to deal with shame yet, let me show you how it can benefit YOU personally! Let's start with something that applies to all of us. Do you know that dealing with your shame and healing old wounds will make you a better friend? Do you humiliate your friends sometimes? Be honest with yourself please. Remember, there's no shame in being human. We all make mistakes. Shame can cause you to lash out in anger or frustration to cover your own shame. Do you want to be friends with someone like that? I don't think so. Those kinds of people are not fun to be around. Do you turn to a secret addiction and find yourself isolating afterwards? When I struggled with emotional binge-eating to numb my pain, I would isolate for days afterwards. I was ashamed to be around people. I wouldn't even respond to text messages. I'm going to guess that on some of those occasions, my friends would have used a kind word or encouragement, but I hadn't made myself available to them. Do you relate to *I'm a burden to others?* This one might surprise you, but if you never reach out for help yourself, then your friends would be less likely to reach out to you. Do you catch yourself worrying about what others will think if they really knew you, and therefore, keep your distance from people? Do you know that if you aren't vulnerable, people will most likely not open up to you either? We all need safe people to talk to, process with, and do life with. Don't let fear keep you from being the friend that is authentic, real, always willing to lend a helping hand, and is kind and gentle. The world needs more safe people, and you could be that person to someone.

Not only will dealing with shame make you a better friend, but also, a better employee. Let's look at the following questions and see if any of them resonate with you. Place a check in the boxes that you can relate to on some level or another.

- ☐ Do you find yourself not able to ask for help when you are stuck on a project at work?
- ☐ Do you freeze up when your administrator comes into your classroom to observe you?
- ☐ Are you a team lead that finds yourself pushing your team too hard and expecting perfection out of them?
- ☐ Do you struggle to speak up when someone at work asks you to lie to the boss to cover up something?
- ☐ Are you afraid to take on new projects out of fear of not being good at it, so you don't even try? Thus, not being qualified later on for a promotion.
- ☐ Do you find yourself criticizing others who you think are a threat to you, so you can feel better about yourself?

If you answered yes to any of the above, there's a good chance that shame is the root behind it. In addition, you may be able to easily see how dealing with the shame could make you a better employee, but let's dig a little deeper together. Let's start with the first question and work our way down. If you never ask questions, how can you learn, much less, grow? I'm not saying you are to ask questions all the time, but there's always someone who knows something we don't that we can learn from. This will allow us to grow and become an even better employee. If you freeze up every time someone walks in your room as a teacher (if you're a teacher, you know it seems like someone is in there all the time), will you be able to give your best lesson and instruction to the students? I know I wasn't. Are you patient with them in those moments? I know I wasn't. Those were the moments I'd often be impatient with them. Do you know why? Because I wanted everything to be perfect in order to keep my shame hidden. I didn't want to be criticized when whoever it was in the room provided their feedback. But why? After all, I'm human. Of course, I won't do any lesson perfectly whether someone is in the classroom or not, but having someone there to pick it apart made me feel the pressure more. The more pressure I felt, the more I expected perfection out of my students and myself; especially as students start acting up at the same exact time someone walks in — well, my fellow teachers know this.

In truth, it's good to give your best at work and to want the best out of your team. But let's be honest, we all know that this can be taken too far sometimes. Do you want to work for a grumpy, critical, and impatient boss? I know I don't! It's no fun! If you are the team lead, you get to be the kind of leader you'd want to work under, but if shame is activated, it's going to be hard. If you're too hard on your team, they can just end up frustrated and defeated. Do you think this will lead them to put out their best work? Probably not. Moving on, have you ever seen something at work you know wasn't right, but kept your mouth shut? This is so easy to do, but I know if someone saw me being mistreated, I'd hope they'd speak up in my favor. Has someone at work asked you to lie? I know that has happened to me. It's uncomfortable, but in the long run, it's always best to be honest.

One time, I was asked to sign a form, saying that we had raised X amount of money. I couldn't do that because see I knew we had asked for donations and later found out we weren't supposed to do that. So, respectfully, I said, "I'm not able to sign it because I know we didn't fundraise for the money." I was already excluded on the team and this just made matters worse. But ultimately, I had a clean conscience and knew that there would be nothing to catch up with me in the future. I didn't have to keep watching my back or keep living in fear at work in anticipation of when this lie would come back to haunt me. I had more energy to focus and give to my students. Do you find yourself not signing up for a class at work because there's a test, and you're afraid you won't pass it? If you face your fears and let yourself, take on new projects or sign up for classes that could advance your skills, this will make you a better employee and a great asset to your boss. It could also set you up for bigger things down the road. You'll never know if you don't try. Last but not least, do you find yourself criticizing and putting other employees down? Especially the ones that seem like a threat to you? I get that, but do you think that will make you the best employee and asset to the company? If your boss has to choose one person to let go because of budget cuts and you and your co-worker have the same skill-set, do you think he's going to choose the one with an encouraging and positive attitude — the one who builds up his other employees? Or you, the one who tears your fellow co-workers down.

We all are a part of a family one way or another. We've either grown up in one or are raising one. Some of us grew up in fantastic families with lots of great things to pass on to our own kiddos. The rest of us grew up in less than healthy families. And if we haven't dealt with our shame and stopped generational cycles, we will pass on what our parents taught us. Whichever group you find yourself in, let's take the good and leave the bad. Let's process the wounds so we can be more whole, become healthier individuals and in turn, be better parents. I think almost every parent desires to be a good parent.

I don't think any parent sets out to be a *bad* parent. And let's face it, no matter how healthy you are, you'll make mistakes as a parent too. Remember, you're human and humans make mistakes. It's okay, there's no shame in making mistakes. My former counselor, Damaris, once told me that it's not about not making mistakes, it's about the repair. Children are resilient and are usually so forgiving! So, if you deal with your shame, you can be the kind of parent who admits to making a mistake, apologizes and asks forgiveness, thus repairing the break with the child. By so doing, you will avoid transferring your shame onto them with criticism and blame. If you are a parent who has dealt with shame, you won't have to ask your kids to keep secrets that will put them in an uncomfortable position; secrets that will possibly be the cause for a root of shame in their life. This shame can get a foothold and start to grow. In addition, you will most likely be patient and gentle with them, rather than angry and frustrated, because you won't have any unhealthy shame to cover for. To wrap this up, one of the best gifts you can give your children is the gift of being fully present. If you have dealt with your unhealthy shame you won't have to isolate and hide from your children. You will also have more emotional energy to give them, because the unhealthy shame won't always be running in the background, slowly draining your emotional battery.

    Now, a lot of what has already been said can be repeated for how dealing with shame can make you a better spouse. You'll be less likely to criticize and blame your spouse. You'll have more grace to give. You're also less likely to transfer your shame onto them. And one of the biggest benefits to your marriage is that you'll be able to be fully known and fully loved, leading to deeper intimacy and connection in marriage.

I hope by now you see the urgency of dealing with your shame, no matter how scary it sounds. I know it can be terrifying! I've been there. I think by now, you can see how dealing with toxic shame will make you a better father, mother, friend, spouse, employee, sister, brother… the list goes on and on. I think it's important to remind you that your *garden* might even begin to get more torn up for a while. I don't say this to scare you, but so you are prepared and not taken off guard. You might even start to think, "I never should have started this garden renovation, because now, it's much worse than before, and I'm not sure I even know how to make it back to the way it was before." But trust me, as someone who has walked the scary garden of the heart renovation on multiple points in my journey, the dust always settles, and the beauty that comes out on the other side is even better than the garden was before. Hang with me. In the next chapter, we'll start finding out how to start digging up the garden of our hearts to become more whole, free, and more beautiful than ever before.

Action Steps—Be brave this week and try sharing something personal with a safe friend. How do I know if a friend is safe you ask? Let me give you a few points of what to look for in someone safe. If you don't have someone safe, please start praying for God to bring someone safe to start sharing with.

Characteristics of safe people: [1]

- They love and accept you as you are, not as you ought to be.
- They don't condemn or judge you.
- They speak the truth in love and encourage you to grow.
- They aren't defensive; rather, they are open to feedback.
- They can admit their own weaknesses.
- They don't demand trust.
- They are humble, not self-righteous.
- They also grow and work on their own faults.

Let me say a prayer for you before I close out this chapter. Lord, thank you for my friend. Thank you for bringing them this far along in their healing journey. Please give my friend courage to face their fear. Give them courage to be vulnerable with someone safe this week. Give the person they share with words of encouragement, support, and empathy. May my new friend feel your love through their safe friend in a tangible way that they've never felt before. Please show my friend just how much you love them and want to bring them healing in their life. Please let them know they are not alone, that you are with them, among many others, walking in this same journey. In Jesus's name, Amen.

---

1 Meier Clinic. Catalyst Binder.

PART 4

HOW DO I FIND THE ROOT

CHAPTER 6

WATCH YOUR THOUGHTS

According to a study done by psychologists at Queen's University in Canada, the average person has 6200 thoughts per day! [1] Whoa, that's A LOT of thoughts! How often do you even pay attention to your thoughts? Do you take them seriously? You might ask, *Do I even have the power to change them? Do they really matter?* I know I didn't always take my thoughts seriously. I used to think some thoughts were harmless; well, I came to find out later that they weren't really harmless.

The truth of the matter is, what you water grows! What are you growing in the garden of your heart? Are you sowing kindness, humility, gentleness, patience, love, joy, peace and self-control?

Hand painted by Emily Ehe

---

1 News18. "Humans Have Around 6,200 Thoughts in a Single Day, Shows New Study." News18. Last modified July 19, 2020. https://www.news18.com/news/buzz/humans-have-around-6200-thoughts-in-a-single-day-shows-new-study-2723281.html.

If you grew up in a Christian home, I'm sure you've heard at some point or another to "take captive your thoughts," coming from 2 Corinthians 10:5. Or to think on whatever is lovely, pure, right, and true.[2] But if you're anything like me, you were probably not sure how to actually take captive your thoughts. Nor were you always sure how to know if a thought fit into one of those categories of being lovely, pure, right, or true. It was a scripture I knew I was supposed to be acting on, but truthfully, I had no idea how.

I mean, of course, there are the obvious things I knew, like harboring the thought of *murdering* someone — that's obviously not a cool thought. That's a thought that one needs to work on changing. I also knew that cursing in my head didn't fit into any of those categories. But what about the thoughts where I'm ruminating over something hurtful that someone said to me. Or replaying a fight I had with my husband earlier that morning. It's true right, because it happened? So, are my thoughts healthy and God-honoring? Are they healthy?

Those are fantastic questions. I'm glad you asked. Let's start first with each word in Philippians 4:8 and break it down, then we'll move into how science backs this up.

- Lovely - Synonyms for lovely are beautiful, stunning, appealing, alluring, exquisite.
- Pure - Synonyms for pure are true, undiluted, flawless, perfect, filtered.
- Right - Synonyms for right are correct, accurate, exact, precise, and unerring.

---

2   Philippians 4:8

- True - Synonyms for true are genuine, authentic, real, fact based, and valid.
- Noble - Synonyms for noble are exceptional, wonderful, first rate, virtuous, and uncorrupted.
- Admirable - Synonyms for admirable are commendable, praiseworthy, exemplary, outstanding, and magnificent.
- Excellent - Synonyms for excellent are outstanding, superb, tremendous, mind-blowing, and marvelous.
- Worthy of Praise -What thoughts are worthy of praise? Will someone be proud of you if you share your thoughts with them? Do they match God, His ways, and His best plan and guidance for your life? You can be certain that if your thoughts align with Him, then it's safe for you to think on.

Let's go back to a scenario posed above and see if we can decide together on whether replaying a fight I had with my husband, all day long, is taking control of my thoughts or not. To clarify further, let's flesh out this example a little bit and give you a glimpse of what's happening in my head on days when we fight. My thinking looks a little like this, *I'm making so much progress, why can't he recognize it and appreciate it. Why can't he just get it together? It didn't take me this long to figure out my part. I can't believe we're back here again. This is annoying. It's going to affect my whole week and set me behind again. It's going to wear me out emotionally. (Insert anger about it here). I'm going to go to the bedroom. I'll shut the door and stay there all night. I'm not coming out, not even to cook dinner. He doesn't deserve it for treating me this way again.* It's a bit embarrassing to admit, but I had similar thinking to this on many different occasions. Yes, I had lots of stinkin' thinkin' and pride to root out! But little by little, with God's help I've come a long way.

Now, let's go back up to our adjectives — the list of healthy and God-honoring thinking. Are the thoughts above alluring and appealing to anyone? Nope. Is my thinking flawless, filtered, exact, and precise? Nope. There are probably misunderstandings in there; things he said that I heard incorrectly. I could be guilty of mind-reading (thinking I know what's happening inside his head) or fortune telling (assuming he's going to lay into me again when he gets home). And I'm probably not being very rational or logical when I'm heated and my emotions are high. I'm focusing on one person — myself. Is all of what I'm thinking true? Most likely not. I'm usually making predictions about the future, based off my past experiences with him. While it makes sense and seems probable, I truly don't know for sure what will happen until it happens. Is anything commendable or praiseworthy in my thinking? Nope. I don't think anyone would give me a complement for such thinking. Are the thoughts I'm thinking mind-blowing and superb? Nope again. Are my thoughts on God and His promises? Nope.

You are probably saying, *okay great. I see what you're saying, but I'm not a Christ follower and I don't really buy all that Bible stuff. So, I don't have to do this.* Thanks for being honest with me. No, you don't *have* to apply any of this. But your mental and physical health will thank you if you do. Let's look at it from the angle of science and see where you're at after that.

Did you know that 75-98 percent of mental, physical, and behavioral illnesses come from your thought process? [3] A disclaimer here. I am not a scientist or researcher. I'm not an expert in the brain and how it works. But I do enjoy reading and learning about it. And in the past couple years, I've learned via reading how important our thinking is for our mental and physical health. The statistic above shows us that. If you're a skeptic and say *okay those numbers are SUPER high. I don't believe that.* I understand and I hear you. Even *if* the percentages are off, it shows that our thinking has a *huge impact* on our life. Toxic thinking creates toxic neuropathways and toxic brain trees, as Dr. Caroline Leaf always calls them. Whereas, healthy thinking creates healthy neuropathways and healthy brain trees. Our thinking can either turn off or turn on proteins in our brain, which is mind-blowing to me! I don't think anyone would deny the fact that the kind of thinking I shared above, in my example, would create stress. Stress releases cortisol, and over time, excess cortisol in the body can lead to health problems. Studies have shown that toxic thinking can lead to inflammation in the body. I have done my best to give you a brief summary of it here, but if you're looking for more information, please check out Dr. Caroline Leaf's book *Switch on your Brain*. She has done tons of research on the brain over the past 3 decades. But here's my stab at summarizing what I have learned over the last couple years on the science around the importance of our thinking.

I don't know about you, but personally, I like it when someone practically shows me what they are talking about and what it would look like. Let's take our example of stinkin' thinkin' above and show

---

[3] Leaf, Caroline. Switch On Your Brain: The Key to Peak Happiness, Thinking, and Health. Ada: Baker Books, 2013: pg 33

the flip side. *This is frustrating, but it's not the end of the world. I have a choice. I can't control everything that happens to me in life, but I CAN control my response to it. I know my husband didn't intentionally speak harsh words to me. He must be going through something, or I probably said something disrespectful. This fight will set me back, but this is not a surprise to God. He will give me strength to get through it. Let me keep my focus in the present and not start worrying about tomorrow. I am hurt by my husband's words, but I am choosing to believe the best, until I have all the facts and have heard his side. I know it's scary, but I don't need to self-protect and predict what will happen when he comes home. I can greet him with a hello and in gentleness and humility, ask him if we can talk through what happened this morning, because the Lord is fighting for me. I'm choosing wisdom over my flesh. Lord, help me.*

Can you see the difference? Which scenario has higher stress levels? The first one, right? Are we creating healthy pathways in the garden of our brain? Or toxic ones? Let's go back to our list, apply the adjectives to our scenario and see if they match up!

Are the thoughts above alluring and appealing to anyone? I know I'd be drawn to someone who has such thought process. I think that after a fight, my husband would be drawn to me if my thinking is like this. Is my thinking flawless, filtered, exact and precise? It looks like I'm filtering my thinking and not allowing toxic thoughts in, by displacing them with truth. I assume the best until I have all the facts, outside of the heat of the moment, as there are probably misunderstandings from things he said that I heard incorrectly. I'm not a mind-reader (thinking I know what's happening inside his head), neither am I a fortune teller (assuming he's going to lay into me when he gets home).

I'm much more rational and logical. I acknowledge my pain and frustration which is valid, but I'm also focusing on him and realizing he could be going through something; this is where compassion comes in. The summary of this line of thinking is treating him like I'd want to be treated. This level of self-awareness enables me to have compassion and empathy for him. Is all of what I'm thinking true? I don't see any lies. I see kindness and compassion towards myself and my husband. I'm believing the best, letting my guard down, and ready to listen and understand what he has to say. I'm not being quick to jump to conclusions. Is anything commendable or praiseworthy in my thinking? I believe so. I believe God would be proud of me for this line of thinking. It matches up with the wisdom in Proverbs on not making my vexation known at once [4] and trying to overlook an insult [5]. Are the thoughts I'm thinking mind-blowing and superb? I think most people would find this mind-blowing. As humans, this is not our natural place to go when someone has hurt or insulted us. Are my thoughts on God and His promises? Yep. I'm comforting and reminding myself of truth that He is with me, He will give me strength and He is fighting for me. He is my shield and protector. I don't have to protect myself.

Where do you think my stress levels are in this scenario? Much lower. Why is that, you ask? Because emotions follow thoughts. If you don't believe me, test it. Each time you notice an emotion or feeling, go back to what you were thinking right before you felt the emotion. I see a drastic difference in my life when I check my stinkin' thinkin' and replace it with truth. Jenni Allen in her book *Get Out of Your*

---

4 Proverbs 12:16
5 Proverbs 17:9

Head gave us a simple phrase that stuck with me. *I have a choice.* [6] Sometimes, in the heat of the moment, things move fast but if I can remember that phrase when I feel my flesh rising, it halts and slows me down. I always endeavor to remember that I have more of a choice than I think I do. I don't have to go back down the well-worn pathway of toxic thinking. I can choose to create new, healthy pathways in the garden of my mind.

This year, I'm studying Proverbs and it's packed with wisdom and nuggets of truth to take with me. One that struck me was Proverbs 14:30 (MSG), "A sound mind makes for a robust body, but runaway emotions corrode the bones." This verse backs up what science and researchers have found. Healthy thinking leads to healthy emotions, which in turn leads to better health and a longer life. The choice is yours. What choice are you going to make today?

"But I can't take captive all my thoughts, Emily. You don't know how many toxic thoughts I have." No, I don't, but I do know I carried boatloads of stinkin' thinkin' with me into adulthood, and it's taken years of work, pulling out those weeds in the garden of my mind that threatened to poison me. Slowly but surely, God is giving me victory in this area. But that doesn't mean that at times, you won't get caught up in it again. Just this week, as I was editing, I got buried under thoughts that fueled strong emotions and threatened to drown me, but I came out victorious! He can and will do the same for you if you let Him. Remember, you are not the exception to the rule, neither am I. Take it one step at a time. One moment at a time. Eventually, all those small steps forward will lead to a giant change in your life.

---

6 Allen, Jennie. *Get Out of Your Head: Stopping the Spiral of Toxic Thoughts.* Waterbrook Press, 2020: pg 40

Each step forward will start to impact your mental and physical state. You didn't get here overnight and you won't get out overnight, but I promise you, it's worth it. Right now, I'm speaking this to myself based on the setback I had, just as much as I'm speaking with you. Remember, we are human and we make mistakes. What we can do is learn from them and try to go forward in a different direction in the future.

Action Steps— Read Philippians 4:8 in 5 different versions and compare them. Ask God for wisdom and insight on how to apply them in your life right now.

CHAPTER 7

LISTEN TO WHAT YOU TELL YOURSELF

You talk to yourself more than anyone else does. Whether you realize it or not, you talk to yourself all day every day inside your head. It's something you probably haven't thought of before because it's more of an automatic response, and the words aren't vocal. I know I hadn't really thought about it that way until a few months ago, but let's think about this. Who is with you everywhere you go? You are! No one follows you to work, then back home, and goes to sleep with you, except you. So, what do you tell yourself? Are you building yourself up or tearing yourself down?

I know for a good part of my life; I was tearing myself down with inner dialogue. Repeating lies to myself over and over because I didn't know they were lies. I thought they were truth. It seemed like God had given me victory over the negative self-talk and lies, and then marriage happened, and I was confused and began to question whether I had ever really grown at all. All the old lies were back. *I'm a failure. I was a terrible daughter and now wife. I can't do this. I'm bad at communicating. I can't do anything right. I'm a mistake. I'm broken. I'll never be fixed. This is going to last forever. I'm going to have to withdraw emotionally to survive and break my commitment to myself.* I wanted to die, and I even asked God to take my life on multiple occasions. It seemed like the only answer to my *problem*. I was buried under lies like these, and it terrified me. I hadn't wanted to die in a long time; the last time I felt that dark was probably in my teenage years. I was beyond terrified to feel it again. I didn't want to numb out, and so I fought hard to keep that commitment to myself, but it didn't look like I was going to be able to keep it. A friend encouraged me during this time with a boxing analogy. She told me that all my previous healing and growth was not lost. But before marriage I was in the amateur rink, fighting against other amateurs and I was starting to get pretty good! I was starting to win all my fights! But at this point, I was no longer fighting against amateurs. Now, I was fighting the big dogs — the professionals, and I was getting beat up!!! But in time, my skill level would be up to par with the professionals, and eventually, I'd be winning those fights again too. This made perfect sense to me, and brought encouragement to my tired, defeated, and terrified heart. To use our garden analogy, I was an onion, and only some of the layers had been peeled; now, it was time to get the core of the onion (which I had thought had already happened, BUT boy was I wrong!).

In the course of all of this, I noticed that my husband never lost hope. He always just said, "we're learning." Almost all the time, he would reassure me, telling me, "It's going to be okay; this will pass." In reality, things looked pretty hopeless to me. He told me he'd choose me all over again time and time again. This baffled me because I wasn't so sure that I would if I had known what I was signing up for. I mean, I knew marriage wasn't happily ever after and I'd heard all my life that marriage is hard, but *hard* sounded like the biggest understatement! It felt more like unending hell that I signed up for!

By now, you're probably wondering, what in the world were you going through? What was happening in your marriage? I wondered that too for a long time because both of us loved Jesus, and we were both pretty easygoing and considerate people. We weren't fighting about money or sex; some of the most common sources of conflict in marriage. We weren't fighting over how the toothpaste should be rolled or which way the toilet paper roll went. We weren't fighting about household chores or how the house should be set up. None of the things I've heard other couples fight about. For this reason, I was so confused and so was he!

He's from Togo and I'm from the U.S. of A., and for some time, we didn't think we were experiencing cultural issues in our relationship until we were married. About a year or so in, I was reminded of hot and cold cultures and their differences, and then the lightbulb went on! I was looking at things from a cold culture perspective and he was looking at things from a warm culture perspective, and neither of us could understand the other, what felt like all of the time! (There were other big communication issues coming into play as well). It was exhausting, I started getting worn out, and I wasn't good holding my boundaries to stay within my limit. Consequently, I started to get reactive in our marriage, as my shame was getting poked at, and by this time, we'd already fallen into bad habits that had to be broken.

What all this showed me was that I was lacking grit and perseverance. However, upon reading books on this, I learned that it could be developed! This was great news! One big thing that I saw missing from my life, keeping me from having grit, was positive self-talk. Leading up to this time, God had been speaking to me a lot about my thinking and so, reading this and seeing how my thinking didn't align showed me that was part of the difference between my husband and I. I had toxic thinking, stemming from toxic shame that was creeping back into my life when my childhood wound was triggered. The situation I experienced in marriage sent the same signals through my body as I experienced in childhood, when I wanted to die. Angela Duckworth in *Grit, The Power of Passion and Perseverance*, said something that jumped out at me. *This seminal experiment proved for the first time that it isn't suffering that leads to hopelessness. It's suffering you think you can't control.*[1] That really resonated with me. My husband had experienced suffering (hard times), growing up, but he didn't experience hopelessness like I did. For example, he lost his father at a young age, wasn't raised by his own mother, didn't start school until he was much older than some of the other kids, and grew up in a lower-class family which meant more work for him and less time to just be a kid, like those he saw around him. However, he always thought he had control in some form or fashion. I, on the other hand, thought I had no control in both childhood and marriage. I thought I was stuck. As you can see his mindset was different than mine, which drastically changed our outlook.

Shortly after, I read *Get Out of Your Head* by Jenni Allen, and something she said stuck with me. *I have a choice.*[2] I had to think about that for a moment. I recalled what I had learned about how my emotions follow my thinking, and I began to see that she was right. I thought back on different fights where I reacted and could pinpoint

---

1 Page 172
2 Allen, Jennie. *Get Out of Your Head: Stopping the Spiral of Toxic Thoughts.* Waterbrook Press, 2020: pg 40

how my thoughts came first; that caused me to spin into a fury of strong emotions.

I will never forget the first time my husband was throwing flesh balls at me after this revelation. When in the heat of the moment, I actually remembered, *I have a choice,* right before I started throwing flesh balls back, as I almost always did before this point. It stopped me in my tracks. I told him something like, *I don't want to fight with you. I have a choice. I'll be back.* I put on my running shoes, and off for a run I went. Wow! That felt great! I was in charge of my thoughts, and that in turn was controlling my emotions! I'd never experienced it like that on such a *professional* boxer level. Now, don't go thinking my life transformed right there. Nope, it was still burdened with a lot of ups and downs, as is often the case with progress; it's one step forward and two steps back. That's about what it looked like for me, except maybe more like five steps backwards and one step forward. Nonetheless slowly but surely, I was seeing the fruits of changing my toxic thinking.

Each time I caught my thinking, before it sped off, leaving in me in the dust, I saw that I had control in the midst of my *suffering* to some extent. In times when I thought I didn't have control in the midst of my *suffering*, I'd see the shift. I'd fall back into the thinking, *This nasty fighting is still happening after two years. It's always going to be this way. I can't do this anymore.* I kept seeing over and over, in this context the truth, how I couldn't control my circumstances, but that I could control how I responded to them. But, WOW, it is hard, and it definitely takes work, practice and healing!

When I reflect back on the moments, where I spun out and ended up back in my 'dark hole,' as I started calling the horrible, dark, hopeless place, the difference *always* had to do with my thinking. Now, I know it's not recommended to use words like *always* and *never*, because they are rarely true. But in this instance, it's true. When I caught the thought out of the gate, I was much more successful in staying calm, and I was also in a much healthier place. Always. The tricky part is, catching that thought and reconceptualizing it in the heat of the moment. But with time, practice, patience, and healing, IT. IS. POSSIBLE.

Back a few months ago, my husband and I hit a rough patch again. It was back to every other day fighting. I was exhausted, and I found myself slipping back into the *I can't do this anymore* line of thought. It was sneaky. I'd hear the thought in my head, and without really stopping to correct it, I would keep going on with my day. I knew I had to take the thought seriously, but I didn't. Before I knew it, I was saying it more consistently, on and off for two weeks. You know what happened? I started getting reactive again, and going off on my husband again. You know what happened as soon as I changed my stinkin' thinkin'? You guessed it! I started being calmer and healthier in the heat of the moment.

I can hear you saying, *That's great and all. But what do I change my thinking to? I really can't do this anymore. I'm tired, worn out and beat down.*

How about reframing it to something like this?

I'm afraid that I can't do this anymore.

"I have given you everything you need for life and godliness. When you are weak, I am strong. Come to me and I will give you rest."³

If you're like me, you might still be a little lost on how to do that though. What I've come to learn is, breathing is powerful. So, sometimes, when my mind is racing 1000 miles per hour, I just go to our bedroom, close the door, sit on the floor, hide behind the bed and breathe. In 4, hold 7 and breathe out for 8. Or, breathe in for 7 and out for 11. There are lots of different breathing techniques out there, if you want to go looking. But these are the two that I often use. And then I start saying out loud, while tapping the fleshy part of the palm of my hand, *I deeply and completely accept myself even when my husband doesn't. I deeply and completely accept myself even when I slip up and yell at my husband again. I deeply and completely accept myself even when I'm tired and beat down. I deeply and completely accept myself even when I think I can't do it anymore.*

Once my mind is calmer, I can put on music that calms me and reminds me of truth; songs like *Fighting for Me* by Riley Clemmons, *Wanted* by Danny Gokey, *New Today* by Micah Tyler, *I'm Leaning on You* by David Crowder, *Clean* by Natalie Grant, *I Am Loved* by Mack Brock, *Over and Over* by Riley Clemmons, and many more. These are just a few of my favorites, just in case you need a place to start. Oftentimes, listening to music is all I can do, so I just lay on the bed, relax, and listen. Oftentimes, I cry and pray while listening.

When I'm relaxed and calm, I usually start knitting while watching a show or listening to a podcast. That gives me something to

---

3   2 Corinthians 12: 10-11; Matthew 11:28

stay busy with, so my thoughts don't take over again and get the best of me. Or if there are dishes to do, I'll go do them while listening to music. It's important to note that the positive self-talk doesn't stop. It continues *while* listening to music, *while* going for a power walk, *while* doing dishes, etc. Those pathways of toxic unhealthy thinking are still well worn in my brain, and it doesn't come as naturally for me as I'd like *yet*. But there's growth! Progress over perfection! That's what I'm striving for! How about you? Something I ask myself often is, *Is there upward movement?* The answer to that for me is yes. Forward movement is all I can ask for in myself or anyone else. I didn't get here overnight, and so I won't get out overnight. When I shift my thinking from how far I have left to go to how happy I am to see progress and celebrate it, this helps reset me and bring my motivation back. So, what do you say? Do you want to join me on this journey towards progress, no matter how big or small? We can work on this together. I'm not where I want to be on this yet either.

    What does positive self-talk look like while you're listening to music or on a power walk? I'm glad you asked. It looks different every time. Here's an example of a recent power walk I was on. I was furious with my husband over something. I was on my powerwalk, and 10 minutes in, I realized my thinkin' was stinkin' and that I had a choice to stop it. So, I started talking to myself, *He didn't give you a time to come back together, which is frustrating. You've asked him to please do that in the past and he didn't say no, leading you to think he would respect your request. He didn't, and that doesn't feel nice. This has been happening so much, so I get that. I understand. However, instead of focusing on what he didn't do, let's shift to what he did do. I'm grateful that he asked for a break, because this is a rare occurrence. That shows growth. Remember, growth takes time. It's not going to happen all at once. He didn't do it on purpose. I'm sure in the heat of the moment, he just wasn't able to process it, and old habits of lashing out when I asked for a time slipped back in. It's going to be okay. Once we both calm down, we'll talk about what happened, hear both sides and all will be okay. This is frustrating, but it's not the end of the world.*

What helped me to figure out *how* to practice positive self-talk on myself was thinking through how I talked to my students, as I was a teacher of Pre-K at that time. It made it super practical and tangible for me, and it really helped me see that what I did for my students, I needed to do for myself as well. It gave me a litmus test to check where I was at. If I wouldn't talk like that to my students, then I don't want to be talking like that to myself. Another way to look at it is to think about how you would like someone would talk to you in that moment, and then practice that on yourself. Acknowledge what you're going through. Speak kindly, gently, and softly to yourself. And give yourself *lots* of grace. You're human. You're learning. You're going to make mistakes. You're not going to do it perfectly the first time. But *celebrate* all those little wins along the way, and one day, if you keep at it, those little wins will add up to big wins.

I want to note here that the best time to catch your self-talk is *right away*. If you catch it as soon as it starts forming in your mind, it'll be a lot easier to shift your thinking and the emotions that follow. In my experience, once I land in my 'black hole' as I call it, it's like trying to move a semi-truck with my bare hands. It is almost impossible to budge. But like any muscle you work or any skill you learn, the more you do it, the easier it gets and the more natural it comes.

Before we close, I want to give a few examples of thinking that can be shifted to give you a framework to use if you need it.

I'm a failure → I'm learning. I'm human and I make mistakes. This mistake doesn't define me.

I'm worthless (mistake, broken, etc.) → God says I'm fearfully and wonderfully made. I'm his masterpiece. A masterpiece is a stunning work of art. We'd never call a masterpiece in art worthless, a failure, a mistake, etc., so why do I think I am? I want to be kind to myself.

I can't do this → This is hard. I don't need to feel bad if I can't do it yet.

I'm afraid of failing miserably, as everyone will see → Failure doesn't define me. I'm human and I make mistakes. It won't be fun if I fail my presentation in front of the class, but this doesn't define me. I can learn from my failure and use it to do better next time. God can work *all* things for good, even my weaknesses or mistakes.

Action Steps—Pay attention to your inner dialogue as you go, throughout your day. Pause when you catch yourself being judgmental or hard on yourself. Reconceptualize the thought into a healthy and true thought. A good guideline to follow is, "if you wouldn't say it to someone else, then you probably shouldn't say it to yourself."

You've got this! I believe in you! Next time, we'll start working together on healing the root, so the trigger is being hit less, and thus, becomes less prominent. Now, doesn't that sound wonderful?

In case that isn't enough motivation for you, let me show you some amazing health benefits if you switch from negative self-talk to positive self-talk. Researchers continue to show that there are tangible, physical benefits to shifting our thinking:

- Increased lifespan.
- Lower rates of depression.
- Lower levels of distress.
- Greater resistance to the common cold.
- Better psychological and physical well-being.
- Better cardiovascular health, and reduced risk of death from cardiovascular disease.
- Better coping skills during hardships and times of stress. [4]

This is not a complete list, but gives you an idea of just how impactful positive self-dialogue can be in all aspects of our life.

---

[4] "How to Stop Negative Self-talk." Mayo Clinic. Last modified January 21, 2020. https://www.mayoclinic.org/healthy-lifestyle/stress-management/in-depth/positive-thinking/art-20043950.

PART 5

HOW DO I HEAL FROM TOXIC SHAME?

CHAPTER 8

EXPOSE IT

Humans are hardwired to connect: Lack of connections alters our brain! Did you know that? The part of your brain that activates when you feel rejected is the same part of your brain that activates with physical pain. Maybe that's why rejection is so painful? [1]

If we didn't know that before March of 2020, I think we all know that now. I think most of us now agree on just how important human interaction is. We've all heard how cases of depression have spiked during the lockdown. We've had to find creative ways to get human interaction during these unprecedented times. That's because we weren't wired to live in isolation. We were wired for human interactions. We are better together. But let's look at the science behind that, find out why it's so important, and what happens when human interaction is absent.

Studies have been done on babies who receive human contact and those who don't. It isn't good for those little babies who aren't held, touched, and talked to. Children who haven't had necessary physical and emotional attention are at a higher risk of behavioral,

---
1 "Humans Are Hardwired for Connection? Neurobiology 101 for Parents, Educators, Practitioners and the General Public." Wellesley Centers for Women. Accessed December 11, 2021. https://www.wcwonline.org/Earlier/humans-are-hardwired-for-connection-neurobiology-101-for-parents-educators-practitioners-and-the-general-public.

social, and emotional problems. Their brains undergo changes that affect them into adulthood. A study done in Romania in the 1980's showed children ages 6-12 who had been in orphanages for more than eight months had higher levels of cortisol and different levels of oxytocin than children raised by parents. Even after being adopted and in a family home for 3 years, it didn't completely override their early years of neglect.

On the flip side, we've known for a long time that skin-to-skin contact is important for babies. That's why babies are often handed to their mothers just after being born for skin-to-skin contact. I'm sure we've all seen the pictures of a dad holding his baby on his shirtless body for skin-to-skin time with his new born child. But are you aware of all the reasons behind it? I know I didn't until I was doing my research for this chapter.

Benefits to a newborn: It helps them cry less and sleep better. Studies show that their brain development is facilitated with physical touch. These babies are more responsive to the mother during their first few months of life, and will recognize their mothers earlier. It works the same way with fathers too. Not only does this skin-to-skin contact benefit the baby, but also, the mother. It reduces their stress level and decreases the possibility of depression. Powerful, huh? [2]

Additionally, there have been studies on loneliness and social isolation in adults. The results have shown that loneliness and isolation pose huge health risks for adults too. It can put them at a 50% increase

---

[2] Harmon, Katherine. "How Important Is Physical Contact with Your Infant?" Scientific American. Last modified May 6, 2010. https://www.scientificamerican.com/article/infant-touch/.

for dementia (about 50% higher), a 29% increase for heart disease, and an increased risk of depression, anxiety, and suicide. [3]

Science backs up what God has to say in His Word too. In Genesis 2:18, he says, "It is not good that man should be alone: I will make him a helper, fit for him." One of my favorite reminders of this truth is in Proverbs 18:1, "Whoever isolates himself seeks his own desire: he breaks out against all sound judgment." I still remember when I heard of this verse in Proverbs, about 7 years ago. I had no idea that the Bible talked specifically about isolation. I had been known to isolate in certain seasons of my life when my shame would rear its ugly head. When I looked at what that verse had to say and reflected on my times of isolation, I saw that play out. When I was in isolation, I was not looking out for the desires of others, only myself. I wasn't doing things for others. My focus was turned inward. When I was at work during those times, I would just be waiting for the day to end, so I could go back into hiding before someone 'uncovered' my shame. Evidently, I was seeking after my own desire. I could also see how it went against all sound judgment by looking at my own life too. I saw how isolation fueled my shame. When I was in seasons of emotional binge-eating, it would just allow that monster to grow as well. However, when I got courageous enough to tell my good friend Maggie - one of the safest people I know - that I was struggling with emotional binge-eating, the shame and hold it had on me began to loosen its grip. Until one day its viny fingers no longer held any power over me.

---

[3] "Loneliness and Social Isolation Linked to Serious Health Conditions." Centers for Disease Control and Prevention. Last modified April 30, 2021. https://www.cdc.gov/aging/publications/features/lonely-older-adults.html.

I love what Brené Brown says on some of her quote cards, "Daring greatly means the courage to be vulnerable, it means to show up and be seen. To ask for what you need. To talk about how you're feeling. To have the hard conversations." It takes courage to be vulnerable. Courage doesn't mean the absence of fear; rather, it is facing the fear and not letting the fear stop you or hold you back. It takes courage to be vulnerable, but it's so worth it. Another great quote by Brené Brown is on vulnerability. On another of her quote cards she says, "Vulnerability is not winning or losing. It's having the courage to show up when you can't control the outcome." Truth! Hopefully, you're sharing with safe people who will speak truth in love, people who will encourage and support you, but there will probably be times the outcome would not be as you hoped. I know the more I grow in vulnerability, the easier it gets, but sometimes, people - even safe people - don't always respond the way we'd hope, and this can leave us feeling vulnerable. Or, as I like to say, 'naked and exposed.' Sometimes, I will share something vulnerable with my husband and he won't say much. I hate that feeling, but I've learned to ask for what I need in those moments. It's a risk, but a risk that I've learned is worth taking. That's when I tell my husband, "I was just vulnerable with you, and now I feel naked and exposed by the side of the road." I can tell that he mostly doesn't really get what I'm saying, but if you've experienced toxic shame, I'm guessing you can relate.

Group therapy shows the power of connection and relationships too. Studies show just how powerful group therapy can be. According to Dr. Coburn, a man I met in a program I went through in summer 2020, group therapy is more effective than individual counseling.

Among the reasons why it's so powerful include: it can reduce stigma, isolation, and wrong thinking such as, *I'm the only one*. Seeing peers change and grow can be catalysts and agents for others in the group, because *if they can learn to feel better and cope, then so can I.* [4]

But what if exposing my shame increases the very shame, I don't want exposed? It very well might. Not what you want to hear, I know. But I'm going to bet that in most cases, if you are sharing with safe people, it will actually be encouraging. I recall a few years back, when I shared something with a group of safe ladies; something I had never shared before. It was terrifying. I had no idea how they'd respond. Maybe what I thought was true, but hearing it would be hard. On the other hand, I also knew that if I opened up and was honest, maybe they could encourage me on the issue. And encourage me, they did! I was humbled and blown away! We are not designed to be in isolation. We are better together. When we are down, others can lift us up.

Since we're working to reconceptualize our thinking instead of asking the question, *but what if exposing my shame increases the very shame, I don't want exposed?* why don't you ask yourself the question, *I know it's terrifying to think about, but what if exposing my shame brings healing and freedom?* James 5:16 says, "Therefore confess your sins to one another and pray for one another, that you may be healed. The prayer of a righteous person has great power as it is working." That you may be healed! That sounds worth it to me! It appears the benefits far outweighs the costs. I must add that you don't confess to just anyone though, and don't confess to everyone. Find a few safe

---

4 "Power in Numbers." Https://www.apa.org. Accessed December 11, 2021. https://www.apa.org/monitor/2012/11/power.

people who will speak the truth to you in love, encourage, and show you grace.

I attended a program this summer, where we learned about shame and how it works. Something I heard there stuck with me. They said there are two things to heal shame. Expose it: Acknowledge the fact that it's there and talk about it. The second was to give yourself and others permission to be human. In the next chapter, we'll talk about what it looks like to give yourself and others permission to be human.

Action Steps—Find one safe person to share something you've never shared with anyone before.

CHAPTER 9

GIVE YOURSELF AND OTHERS PERMISSION TO BE HUMAN

Oxford Dictionary defines human as, "of or characteristic of people, as opposed to God or animals or machines, especially in being susceptible to weaknesses." [1] Synonyms for human are *weak, frail, imperfect, vulnerable, susceptible, and error-prone*. How often have you thought of being human in this way? I know it's not something I have personally thought about often. But it's right there in the definition that we are susceptible to weakness. The synonyms simply tell us that we are error-prone, frail, and imperfect. So, why do we find ourselves trying so hard, exhausting ourselves in a bid to be superhuman and cover all mistakes? Why do we feel the need to always be strong? To never get tired? Why do we think we are failures if we make a mistake? Why do we think we aren't good enough if we can't do everything? Why do we go to subhuman when our humanness is exposed? Shame. But if we heal our shame, we can allow ourselves to simply be in the middle— human.

---

[1] "HUMAN | Definition of HUMAN by Oxford Dictionary on Lexico.com Also Meaning of HUMAN." Lexico Dictionaries | English. Accessed December 14, 2021. https://www.lexico.com/en/definition/human.

Superhuman
Human
Subhuman

It's just simply a part of who we have been ever since the fall, back at the Garden of Eden in Genesis 3. God didn't design us to be imperfect, but it's a part of the consequence of Adam and Eve's choice that has affected every human being since then. God placed Adam and Eve in a beautiful, stunning garden. He gave them one command — just one: "You may surely eat of every tree of the garden, but of the tree of the knowledge of good and evil, you shall not eat, for in the day that you eat of it, you shall surely die." [2] When we disobey God, it brings death. In their case, it did not cause immediate death, but from that point on, they lost the ability to live forever. Adam lived up to 930 years of age. [3] Now, to us, that sounds like forever, because nowadays, most of us don't make it to see 100! Thus, imagining someone living 930 years is hard to fathom! But they were created to not die, and slowly, over the years, people started living less and less years. By the end of Genesis, lifespan had already decreased significantly. Joseph died at 110 years. [4] Death entered the world both physically and spiritually. So, since fallenness and mistakes are a part of who we are now, let yourself off the hook! Allow yourself to be human! There's

---

2 Genesis 2:16-17
3 Genesis 5:5
4 Genesis 31: 26

so much life and freedom to be found here! Not only can it bring a myriad of health benefits, it can also lengthen your life span.

Think back with me to a time when you made a choice that wasn't kind. Maybe you lashed out at your kids with your words. How did that feel internally? Did you feel guilty? Did you feel shame? When I think back to a time where I did something I regret, it doesn't feel nice internally. Oftentimes, I feel guilt, and other times, I feel shame. It's not a fun feeling. It's not a place I would describe as full of life. Internally, it feels more like my *garden* is withering and dying. Now, let's look at the flip side; how do you feel when you make a choice that *is* kind and loving? What do you feel internally? Personally, I feel joy and happiness. I get excited when I make the kind and loving choice, even when it's hard. Inside of me, it feels like the garden of my heart is full of life, blooming, and that new shoots are sprouting out of the ground!

Now, let's take this full circle and bring it back to shame. Create a mental picture of how you feel internally, when you are being superhuman. When you have to do a boatload of activities, and you are more of a human doing than a human being, what comes to mind? What do you feel in your body? Exhausted. Tired. Worn out. Drained. What about when you are in the subhuman category? When you are in hiding and thinking you are worthless? What is happening internally? Hopelessness. Fatigue. Misery. Despair. Discouragement. You may feel like you have lead in your body, and are being weighed down. Do any of these resonate with you? Personally, I've resonated with both subhuman and superhuman at various points in my life, and sometimes, I still find myself slipping into them at times. Once I feel like that, I know I have a choice to make, in order to find my way back to being human! What a lifegiving place to live!

Living in the middle, being human, is like sitting in a shaded garden with birds chirping all around you; flowers blooming, a soft breeze blowing on your face and butterflies flitting around you. Close your eyes and join me to imagine what you might be feeling this very moment, sitting in this stunning garden. Calm. Peace. Rest. Quiet. Joy. Happy. Relaxed. All the pleasant peaceful feelings we enjoy, right? *Yes, please tell me how to get there. I want to live in a place like that.* I know it sounds too good to be true. I'm pretty sure you've heard the saying, if it sounds too good to be true, it probably is. That is often the case. But having walked this journey little by little over the past many years, I'm here to tell you it's possible! It's not too good to be true.

What does it look like to live in the middle, human being, space day in and day out? What does it look like practically? Those are questions I'd be asking if I were reading this book. I like practical, tangible and hands on. So, let's dig in!

WHAT IT LOOKS LIKE EVERY DAY TO BE HUMAN

What does it look like in the classroom? Your students go crazy. You start to get so flustered and afraid, you're about to lose your cool with them. It won't be long before your voice is raised — and not just in the stern teacher kind of voice way. Rather, the selfish, "I'm frustrated and you're driving me crazy," kind of way. Stop the noise for a moment inside your head and tell yourself, *it's okay. It's normal to get information overload sometimes with all the noise. I'm human.*

It's a part of being human. It's okay if I don't get through all the material today. I'm human, and sometimes the expectations placed on me aren't very human or realistic. So, I'm going to take myself off the hook, so I can get some of the pressure off my back. Once that's done, you'll be able to say, *"Hey kiddos, all this noise is getting to teacher. Can we take a moment to breathe together to calm ourselves down (*or lower our brain glitter-a fun analogy for kids*)?* This allows you and the kiddos to be human! [5]

I can hear the doubt in your head already — *but I can't stop right in the middle of my lesson and do this. There's not enough time in the day. It won't work.* Trust me, I get it. I've been a teacher, and I've had those same doubts/excuses, so I get you. I hear you. But I had a fantastic mentor who showed me how. I saw firsthand how it worked for her and knew it was only a matter of practice for me to get there; that it wasn't just another unrealistic thing I was being told to do. I saw it was a skill that would just take practice. You're human, remember? It won't happen perfectly the first time, but the more you do it, the better you become. The more the kids do it, the better they get at it and the better they respond to it.

What does it look like as a parent? You wake up late. Baby is cranky. Toddler won't stop asking questions. Second glass of milk is spilled on the floor. You're already running late to get to a doctor's appointment for one of the kiddos. Stop the noise happening around you for a few seconds. Tell yourself *it's okay. This is frustrating, but not the end of the world. I don't want to be late for the doctor's appointment, and I like that. But sometimes, life happens. I'm human, and so is my*

---

5 See examples at end of chapter for more explanation

child. I spilled lots of things on accident as a child, and so will my child. I hated it when my mom yelled at me for doing it. I want to treat my child like I'd want to be treated. I'm going to breathe in and out slowly, a few times. I'm going to let myself off the hook. It's okay to be late. Sometimes, it's out of my control. Or I can choose to just leave the spilled milk and clean it up when we get back. It's not the end of the world for milk to sit spilled on the floor.* Now that you are calmer, depending on your choice, you can say something like, *It's okay sweetie. Accidents happen. We're running late for the doctor's appointment so let's just be careful not to step on it. We'll clean it up when we get back. Will you go get your shoes please? Thanks!*

What does it look like as a spouse? Spouse does that thing that irritates you again. You want to lash out and be impatient with them. Take a few seconds and breathe, while talking to yourself. *I have a choice. I don't have to respond in frustration. My spouse is human and I'm human. Therefore, things he or she does will irritate me, but I can choose to respond in love. I can choose to treat them as I'd want to be treated. I can choose to believe the best — that he or she isn't doing it to irritate me. We are just different, and as a result, we don't always understand each other and find things that the other does as irritating. It's okay.* Slowing down to think before you speak and have healthy inner dialogue will allow you to now respond to them in love, using words that shower grace, kindness, compassion, and understanding. It will allow you to consider your spouse as more important than yourself. Realize that it's your flesh and things not going the way you want or expect that are most likely causing the irritation. When I choose to act in irritation, I'm indirectly saying that my needs, wants, desires, or expectations are more important than my spouse's.

If you are a Christ-follower, God calls us to, "Do nothing from selfish ambition or conceit, but in humility, count others more significant than yourself." [6]. Wow! Not easy, but with God's help, it's possible! And if you'll notice, He doesn't give exception clauses like, when they are easy to love, when they respect you, when they don't lash out in anger, or only when they don't say hurtful words. Nope. He says to do it! Period.

What does it look like as a neighbor? A neighbor's yard guy blows leaves into your yard. *That's frustrating, but it's not the end of the world. I don't like it, but we haven't even done our leaves yet, so it's not that big of a deal. If it continues, I can kindly ask him to talk to his yard guy to not do it anymore. I can assume the best of my neighbor and choose to believe it's not personal.*

What does it look like at work? That challenging co-worker comes to your desk to talk. *This person can be frustrating. I'm human, so it's natural to not want to be in a conversation with someone that isn't easy to be around. But no one else in the office talks to them. It can't feel nice to be in their shoes. I can give them a few minutes of my time to show them love. That's what I would want someone to do for me. I wouldn't want to be shunned, just because I'm difficult or a little different.*

How do you expect me to do this? You don't know the kind of neighbor I have. You don't know my significant other. You don't know my co-worker. You're right. I don't. But I know that God's way is always best. His ways aren't there to keep us from having fun; rather, to lead us to life. He doesn't make exceptions, so, neither should you and

---

6   Philippians 2:3-4

I. We can't do this on our own, but with His help and strength, we can! He is our strength! If you don't know him yet as your personal friend and savior, please accept God's free gift to you today! [7] If you have questions, please reach out to me or someone you know who already has a personal relationship with Him. He is the best ever! I can't imagine doing life without Him by my side to guide me, gently set me back on the right track when I get off, and be there for me when no one else is.

    I know that what I'm challenging you to do isn't the easiest path to take. In fact, it's a bumpy path to take at times, but at the end, there is a marvelous garden, waiting for you to do life in it and *just dwell*. The only way to heal shame is to take yourself and others off the hook and to talk to safe people about it. Share it. Expose it.

    Each time you do, it will get a little easier. Remember, you have nothing to prove. What you do or don't do doesn't define you. What people think or say doesn't define you. The more you heal your shame, the more you can rest and get to the marvelous garden of life on the other side, even when there's chaos around you. Because you know that you have nothing to prove as a teacher in that chaotic classroom when someone walks in to observe you, you'll say, *I'm human and the kids are human as well. Sometimes, this is just what our classroom looks like, and it doesn't define me; neither does it define them. It's just a part of being a teacher.*

    What about when your boss falsely accuses you and doesn't listen to your side of the story? Once you deal with your shame, you

---

7 "Why Is Salvation Through Christ Alone?" Crosswalk.com. Last modified February 1, 2021. https://www.crosswalk.com/faith/spiritual-life/why-is-salvation-through-christ-alone.html.

won't have to wrestle with it for long and let it suck the life out of you for days, and even weeks. Instead, it'll be a quick conversation with yourself, and then you'll be able to just rest in the majestic garden and have inner peace because you know, *what she says doesn't define me. It sucks that she thinks that, but what can I do. I don't have to prove myself to her. Just because she thinks it's true, doesn't make it true.*

What about when your spouse grossly misunderstands you, refuses to hear your side, and hurls incredibly harsh, hurtful, and untrue words at you? Or, when your spouse is hurtful with his words and shaming you about a mistake you made or a struggle you have? Or, trying to shame you for something you aren't doing wrong? Yep, even then, once your shame is healed, you can still sit peacefully in that relaxing garden of your heart because you know that you have nothing to prove. What your spouse says doesn't define you. Stinks to be you when your spouse doesn't want to hear your side, but the truth is, you can't make them hear you out. If you've actually done what they are saying, try saying something like, *Yeah, you're right. I did that. My bad. My apologies.* By doing this consistently, your shame will be healed, and you'll avoid being defensive and lashing out in anger, in a bid to hide your own shame. Your toxic shame will be gone. Healed. Dealt with.

And when you experience healthy shame, remember that it's not a bad thing; it's a warning light. It's just reminder that you are human, and you have limits. These days, when I slip up and go all out on my husband again, I just remember that I'm human, therefore I have limits and that, at that particular time, I crossed them. This realization is a flashing light, telling me that I need to make some changes, so, hopefully, I can stay within my limits next time. It's important to note that it's not as easy as it might sound. Sometimes, I try to stay within my limits and my husband doesn't respect it. I'm still trying to figure out how to navigate this, when it's not as cut and dried as it might sound. So, please don't think I have it all figured out. Just like you, I am still on this journey. My neuro-pathways in my brain are still being re-wired and re-routed. The difference now is that when I feel shame, it's just a warning to me that I'm human and I have limits. The toxic voices inside my head don't start to swirl anymore, like they used to. On the rare occasions that they do, when a toxic thought passes through, it's just reminder to me that I'm not where I want to be yet, that I still have more work to do, and I need to keep working on my new skills because I've exceeded my human limits and need to keep working on my boundaries. It gives me the opportunity to step back, see where I slipped up, and gives me energy to set boundaries to help prevent it from happening again. I'm human just like you. *Healing is messy!* Let that sink in. Healing is a lot of ups and downs. It looks a lot like this.

WHAT HEALING LOOKS LIKE

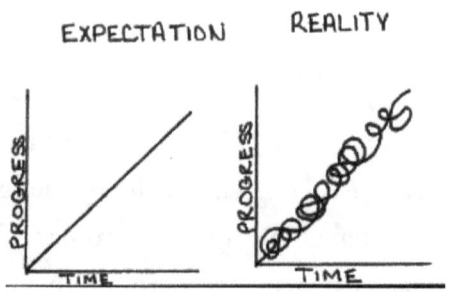

Image drawn by Emily Ehe. Taken from the concept of similar images seen like this over the years.

Let me leave you with this, "Have I not commanded you? Be strong and courageous. Do not be frightened, and do not be dismayed, for the Lord your God is with you wherever you go." [8]God gave this to the Israelites before they made the long journey into the Promised Land. I think we can apply this verse to our own journey of crossing over into the Promised Land in our own lives. In the next chapter, you'll learn what you need to do to keep shame in its proper place and also maintain the growth you've seen in yourself already so far.

Action Steps—Sit and reflect on your day-to-day life. Where are you not allowing yourself to be human? Where are you not allowing others to be human? If we don't deal with your toxic shame, you will continue the cycle of toxic shame in your family and pass it onto the next generation. You have a chance right here and right now to walk over into the *Promised Land,* where there is freedom and life to be found. You have the opportunity to stop generational cycles that have been passed down for years. Please be courageous and take an honest look at your life. What areas do you need to release yourself from pressure and expectations on yourself and others that aren't human?

*In my experience, a visual works better when doing it with kids. It grabs their attention and keeps them engaged throughout the process. A Hoberman Sphere, which can be bought on Amazon, is a plastic ball that expands in and out. This gives a visual to kids to breathe in and out slowly, as the ball goes in and out. YouTube also has lots of great breathing videos for kids as well.

**Brain glitter — This is an analogy I came across when I was a Pre-K teacher. You can fill a small empty water bottle with water

---

8   Joshua 1:9

and glitter. Hot glue the lid shut. Shake it. This is what the human brain looks like, so to speak, when emotions are high. Once all the glitter settles, this is what our brain looks like when we are calm and relaxed, and our emotions are in check. Explain this to the child. They can even shake the bottle when they are upset and then watch the glitter settle; this will in turn calm and help the child settle. Once our *brain glitter* is calm, both children and adults alike, we can think more clearly and logically.

PART 6

HOW DO I MOVE FORWARD & MAINTAIN MY GROWTH?

CHAPTER 10

KEEPING SHAME HEALTHY

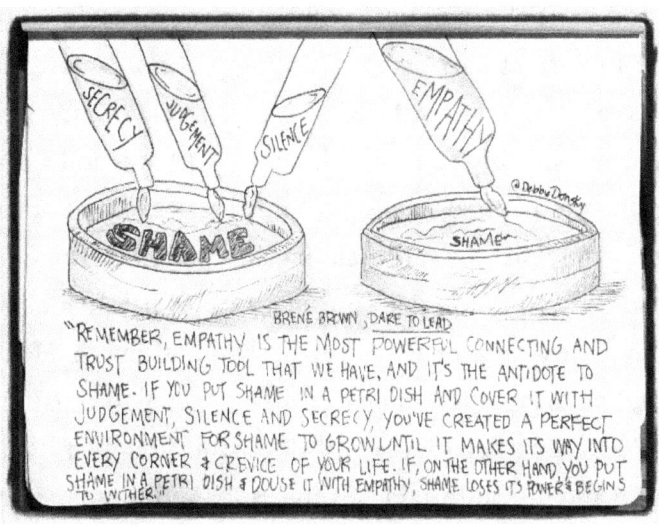

1

This image and quote from Brené Brown, sums up perfectly all we've been talking about up to this point. It shows the three ingredients we need to avoid to keep our shame healthy and in its proper place. Or, to look at it another way, it perfectly demonstrates the one thing we need in order to keep shame from growing and to heal it — empathy. According to Oxford Languages dictionary empathy is the ability to

---
1 https://i1.wp.com/debbiedonsky.com/wp-content/uploads/2018/10/IMG_6241.jpg?fit=2413%2C1775&ssl=1

understand and share the feelings of another. ²You can get empathy from others of course, but you should also give it to yourself. I'll talk more about that in the later part of this chapter.

COMMUNITY

You have learned that you can't keep isolating. You also know what safe people look like now. Perhaps you have some safe friends already; if you don't already know, you should know now that this is vital and an important part of your healing process. Simply talking about shame can heal it. Just last week, I was at my counseling session, and was sharing with my counselor how my husband and I make a great team; how our gifts, strengths, and weaknesses complement each other. I enjoy hosting, and relationship building is one of my strengths. Starting those harder conversations with someone about whether they have a faith or not is my husband's strength. However, at this point, I often get stuck when it comes to taking the relationship to a deeper, less superficial level, if it doesn't just happen naturally. It's really hard and uncomfortable for me. Initially, I thought that this was something *normal* and a part of my wiring. And to some extent, it probably is because some people do have the gift of evangelism. It comes more naturally to them to start up conversations with strangers or friends about God and where they are at; not for me though.

Out of the blue, I found that we were talking about why it is that I struggle with hard, uncomfortable conversations. She was trying to help me find the root behind it and taking the conversation in a

---

2 "EMPATHY English Definition and Meaning | Lexico.com." Lexico Dictionaries | English. Accessed December 11, 2021. https://www.lexico.com/en/definition/empathy.

direction I didn't plan to go, but I went along with it out of a desire see if there was anything there for me to learn from in order to be healthier and more whole. I figured it was worth time to look into and unpack. I'm a firm believer in finding the root of things so we can heal them, dig them up, and plant something healthier in its place. After two sessions, no real answers were found. I experienced some level of fear in those conversations, but that seemed part of being human to me. Although, I know some people don't fear having uncomfortable conversations. I told her it was probably because there was still some toxic shame behind it because I was still in the process of healing all of it at its deepest parts, but in all honesty, I wasn't really sure. After simply *talking* and processing with her, I noticed that I was already freed from some of the twisty vines that were having a grip on me. It's crazy and hard to fathom, but simply talking and sharing with safe people can be healing. It's not something I fully understand, but I have experienced this on many occasions throughout my healing journey. Sharing being healing, not only applies to shame, but healing from traumas and painful events as well.

This talking and processing can happen in various ways. It can happen with a friend or a trusted group of friends. Maybe you need a little more help than a friend can give, and you may also need to seek help in your church or confide in your pastor. It is also possible that some processing will happen as you jump into a Bible study with a group of women and hear how you aren't alone in your struggles. You may even need professional help. There's no shame in that! There's still so much stigma in our culture about going to a counselor or psychiatrist. But let's ask ourselves why we let that hold us back? When you are sick, you go to the doctor. So why is it that when you are in need of some help processing something, you don't go to someone with training and skill in that area to get assistance? A former pastor of mine always said the healthiest people he knows had been through Re:generation. I believe the same can be applied to people in counseling. They are not running from their pain or their problems; rather, they are facing them, finding the root behind their hang-ups, and healing them in the process.

This leads me to another great place to find community. Look for Celebrate Recovery or Re:generation groups meeting in your area. God used Re:generation to bring a lot of healing and freedom to me. He has done the same for many others. Some of the ladies that I met in the course of that program are some of my safest and best friends to this day. It might be a great place for you to start in your journey of finding safe people and a community of people to do life with.

FORGIVING YOURSELF & OTHERS & GOD

Gentleness towards my precious, fragile self as called forth uniquely by God constitutes the core of my gentleness with others.

~Father Adrian von Kahn

It has been said that not forgiving someone is like drinking poison and then waiting for the other person to die. I know, dear friend, forgiveness is hard. It's not easy, but it's worth it. It's similar to shame, in that, when we let go of unforgiveness, it leads to life and peace. It leads to that stunning, relaxing, peaceful garden. Just think with me for a moment on how it feels internally when there's unforgiveness? Restless. Your mind is always going. Your heart might be hard. You might even notice tall walls surrounding the garden of our heart. It probably feels dark, lonely, quiet, and cold in the garden of your heart. Whereas, on the flip side, if there's forgiveness in your heart, what do you think that would be like when you look internally? Quiet. Calm. Peace. Rest. Stillness. A quiet mind. Joy. Happiness. The garden of your heart blooms and flourishes. Life shows up all around you. Sunshine bears down with warmth upon everything within its reach. The person you hurt the most with your unforgiveness is yourself. I can almost hear you from here, *but Emily, you don't know what people have done to me. You don't know how much I have to forgive. I just can't do it!* You're right, dear one. I don't know what you've gone through. But what I do know is that holding onto it will keep you bound in its chains and from truly living. I know it hurts what people have done and said to you. It wasn't right, and my heart hurts for you, but you have to let it out in order for you to heal.

What helps me in moments when I don't want to forgive or when I am struggling to let go is remembering that when I was still far from Christ, God sent His Only Son to die for YOU and ME! [3] We hurt him daily and multiple times in a day. At times, we keep committing the same atrocities over and over. He knew that would happen; he knew of our stubbornness and brokenness, yet, His love was so deep that He still went on to do it. He pardoned and absolved you of YOUR sin, through the death of His Son, so that YOU and I can have relationship

---

3 Romans 5:8

with Him. Sit with that a moment. Let it soak in. Just *how much* God has had to forgive us. If He can forgive us of all that, how can we not forgive others of much smaller debts? Let's let go of all resentments and pardon all that has been done against us, so we can truly live!

There are misunderstandings around forgiveness sometimes, so I want to unpack what forgiveness is and what it's not. I like this definition of *forgive*: To grant pardon for an offense; absolve. 2). To release or give up all claim on account of a debt or obligation. 3). To [give up] resentment against another." [4]We don't use words like pardon or resolve too often, so I want to take a moment to look at synonyms for each to give us a clearer understanding of forgiveness.

Synonyms for absolve and pardon are release, liberate, free, deliver, clear, spare, exempt, let off, overlook, and have mercy on. Wow, that makes it pretty tangible right? Now, I can take these adjectives and then look at my heart to see if I'm harboring unforgiveness or not, pretty clearly

It's also important to note, what forgiveness is not. [5] Forgiveness is *not* excusing sin. God takes sin seriously and hates it. Sin is never okay.

- Forgiveness is not freeing the guilty of a demand for justice. It's transferring the debt to God and allowing Him to give justice in His time and His way.
- Forgiveness is *not* denying your hurt or stuffing your anger. God gets angry at sin too. You need to process through the hurt, pain and anger, and release the resentments to God.
- Forgiveness is not a feeling, and it's not conditional. Corrie

---

4 & 5 Re:generation Workbook. Step 8. Pgs. 44 &53

Ten Boom says it perfectly — "Forgiveness is an act of the will, and the will can function regardless of the temperature of the heart." (If you don't know her story, look it up. Her story is powerful.)

- Forgiveness is *not* forgetting. Do you see forget anywhere above in the definitions for forgiveness, or the synonyms for absolve or pardon? Nope. Don't let people try to shame you for not being able to *forgive and forget* as some people often like to say.
- Forgiveness is *not* trust. Just because you have forgiven someone does not mean you trust them. Your forgiveness towards the other person does not make them trustworthy. Forgiveness is a gift that you give the other person, but trust is earned. Trust can be earned by *consistent* trustworthy behavior.
- Forgiveness is *not* reconciliation. Forgiveness is a transfer of debt to God. It's refusing to hold onto resentment. Reconciliation may or may not be possible, depending on the health and trustworthiness of the other person.

I hope that hearing these misconceptions about forgiveness will make it easier to let go of unforgiveness, so you can stop pouring poison on the garden of your heart. I want to note here that it's okay to say you forgive a person while you are still processing it emotionally. Sometimes, we have the desire to forgive, but we aren't quite there yet. Sometimes, my husband really, really hurts me with his words and actions. I want to forgive him right away, but in my heart, I know that I have not, because I can see and feel it in my actions and words. I'm still processing it emotionally and working through it. Sometimes, it takes me a day or two, depending on how bad the situation was. That's okay. Please don't feel guilt for not being able to forgive as soon as you want. I know it can take time and a conscious choice to keep choosing forgiveness over and over again before it's fully laid to rest. This is merely an appeal to commit to getting to full forgiveness as soon as you can, not letting anything linger, grow and poison the garden of your heart. When we get to the action steps, I'll talk a little bit more about who you may need to forgive.

TELL YOURSELF A NEW STORY

When we deny the story, it defines us. When we own the story, we can write a brave new ending.

~Brené Brown

The stories we tell ourselves have a huge impact on us. Talk to yourself like you would a sweet child. Be tender and gentle with yourself. Encourage yourself. Build yourself up. Celebrate your progress and little wins along the way. Acknowledge your feelings and pain. Empathize with your inner child. Catch those thoughts as soon as possible. Remember, *emotions follow thoughts*. Please don't be hard on yourself when you miss a thought or revert to old ways. Be honest with yourself that it's not fun to go backward; in addition, acknowledge where you see progress in the midst of the chaos. Then use the energy from the shame or guilt you are feeling to take correction, action or set boundaries for yourself next time.

I believe there are two reasons that I'm able to be here right now, writing this book. One is because, years ago, I started changing the story I told myself. I stopped telling myself I was a failure, that I was broken, worthless, and a mistake. I began to believe the truth of what God said about me; that I was fearfully and wonderfully made [6], that I was his masterpiece [7], and that God has good plans for me [8]. Full disclosure, my thinking got majorly challenged when I got into a cross-cultural marriage and I went from the intermediate rink into the professional rink (to go back to my boxing analogy from an earlier chapter). I'll be honest; for a while, in my marriage, when I got dropped off the deep end, I began to have some stinkin' thinkin' but God helped me get back on track, and I stopped telling myself *I'm not strong enough. I can't do this. I'll never be good enough for him.* I replaced those thoughts with truths like *God has given me everything I need for life and godliness. God has not given me a spirit of fear, but of power, love, and a sound mind. Don't grow weary in doing good, for in due season YOU WILL reap, if you don't give up.* God's promises and truth saw me through, and they can do the same for you. He is the same yesterday, today, and forever. He is unchanging.

The second reason is because people believed in me. My husband and a friend told me that they saw me writing a book. Hence, when the opportunity dropped in my lap, I didn't tell myself *No, I can't do that. I'm not good enough with words.* Neither did my shame hold me back. *What about if people criticize me?* That happens to authors and people in the public spotlight. *I'm not strong enough for it. What if people*

---

6 Psalm 139:14
7 Ephesians 2:10
8 Jeremiah 29:11

misunderstand me and then use that misunderstanding against me? How can I survive that? I better just stay quiet. Dealing with my shame has made me stronger and more confident. I have nothing to hide. I know that God has my back and is fighting for me. He is my shield, and where He leads, I will follow. I don't need to self-protect. He is MY SHIELD. Now, I can stop protecting myself, rest assured that my Heavenly Daddy would do it for me. An image I came across when I was struggling to stop self-protecting in my marriage and allow God do it for me comes to mind. This visual seemed like a gift from God to me and I pray it resonates and encourages you too.

This image is done by Kevin Carden. (He has many more that are worth checking out. You can find more of his work on Instagram, Facebook, or via a Google search.).

If I can do it, so can YOU! I'm not an exception to the rule and neither are you! I can imagine some of you right now are saying, *but*

Emily, I can't! Yes, you can. I understand you are tired, worn down, and weary. It might seem like you are drowning in an ocean. I understand it's hard. I understand the road is bumpy. But you can do it. If you can't walk yet, crawl. If you can't crawl, scoot. Do whatever it takes to make that first baby step. In order to act out the steps below, look at what's holding you back so you can get rid of the obstacle and move forward.

Are YOU ready to write a brave new ending to the story called "your life"? You have the tools now; all you need to do is put them into practice! Taking it one step at a time, replacing one lie at a time with truth, finding one friend at a time, sharing your story one brave step in authenticity and vulnerability at a time, and giving yourself and others more grace to be human today than you did yesterday. Before you know it, all those little steps will add up to one giant mountain of progress. Let's look at the action steps for this chapter, but before we do so, I want to encourage you to keep this book by your bed or somewhere within reach. Go back to re-read the places you've highlighted. Keep it handy as a reference, refresher, and source of encouragement.

Tell yourself a new story! Replace your toxic self-talk with positive, healthy, and true self-talk! You got this! I believe in YOU!

Action Steps—Today: Take steps TODAY to find a safe person or community. Maybe research Re:generation or Celebrate Recovery to see if there's a group near you.

Tomorrow: Get away somewhere quiet. Breathe in and out slowly, until your body feels relaxed and your mind is calm. Who do you need to forgive today? Do you hold resentment against someone? Does your tone of voice change when talking about someone? That can be a good litmus test to see if there's resentment in your heart. Are you angry and resentful towards God for something that you blame Him for? Some people say you don't need to forgive yourself, but I think that if you can forgive God or someone else for something, there might be reasons for you to forgive yourself for something you did to yourself that harmed you in some way.

The next day: What's holding you back from being gentle to yourself and telling yourself a new story? Is it someone's voice in your head? Is it you trying to punish yourself for something? Is it shame? Fear? Guilt?

MORE RESOURCES:

https://www.youtube.com/watch?v=1Evwgu369Jw
(Brené Brown on Empathy)

The Soul of Shame by Curt Thompson

Get Out Of Your Head by Jenni Allen

Switch On Your Brain by Dr. Caroline Leaf

www.ingramcontent.com/pod-product-compliance
Lightning Source LLC
LaVergne TN
LVHW051911060526
838200LV00004B/87